Mary and Archie Tisdall have had a life of travel which many would envy. Archie served in the Royal Air Force for 40 years and during this time they lived in such diverse countries as Singapore, Jordan, Libya, Tunisia and Malta. Towards retirement they bought a motorcaravan to enable them to visit further places abroad, principally in western Europe, and gradually they began to write of their experiences for magazines.

They have travelled extensively in Spain, spending numerous winters in the Canary Islands. This resulted, in 1984, in the publication of two guide books: *Tenerife and the Western Canary Islands* and *Gran Canaria and the Eastern Canary Islands.*

Their love of Spain has taken them many times to the Balearic Islands. The outcome is a three-title series on these islands — *Majorca, Menorca* and *Ibiza and Formentera.* Their sixth travel guide describes the beautiful island of *Madeira,* and their seventh book is *The Algarve.*

Archie and Mary Tisdall have two sons, two daughters and five grandchildren and when not travelling they live in Salisbury, Wiltshire.

Acknowledgements

The authors wish to thank the following people and organisations who gave information, directly or indirectly, which was used in the preparation of this book: The Director and Staff the Ministerio de Transportes Turismo y Communicacione, Cabildo Insular de Gran Canaria; Francisco Ortega, Director Patronata de Turismo de Lanzarote, and Elana; Andres Valeron Hernandez, Gerente, Patronata Excmo, Cabildo Insular de Fuerteventura — also Claudia and Olga; The Directors of hotels and *viajes* who gave us so much assistance in Lanzarote and Fuerteventura; also Sharon Alexander of Brittany Ferries and to K.R. Smith of Regency Pictures for the front cover photograph.

Our grateful thanks to Yvonne Messenger, our helpful and patient editor, and to our publisher, Roger Lascelles and Bryn Thomas. Finally we wish to thank our family and friends for their practical help and encouragement.

Front Cover: *Both Lanzarote and Fuerteventura have idyllic beaches for sunbathing and swimming in clear seas. The dark volcanic mountains make an unusual sight against the sand dunes.*

Lanzarote and Fuerteventura

A Travel Guide

Mary and Archie Tisdall

Roger Lascelles, Cartographic and Travel Publisher
47 York Road, Brentford, Middlesex TW8 OQP. Tel: 081-847 0935

Publication Data

Title	Lanzarote and Fuerteventura
Typeface	Phototypeset in Compugraphic Times
Photographs	Front Cover: K.R. Smith (Regency Pictures, 35 Regent Park Tce, Leeds LS6 2AX). Other photographs by the Authors
Index	Jane Thomas
Printing	Kelso Graphics, Kelso, Scotland.
ISBN	0 903909 88 X
Edition	First Jan 1991
Publisher	Roger Lascelles 47 York Road, Brentford, Middlesex, TW8 0QP.

Distribution

Africa:	South Africa —	Faradawn, Box 17161, Hillbrow 2038
Americas:	Canada —	International Travel Maps & Books, P.O. Box 2290, Vancouver BC V6B 3W5
Asia:	India —	English Book Store, 17-L Connaught Circus/P.O. Box 328, New Delhi 110 001
	Singapore —	Graham Brash Pte Ltd., 36-C Prinsep St
Australasia:	Australia —	Rex Publications, 413 Pacific Highway, Artarmon NSW 2064. 428 3566
Europe:	Belgium —	Brussels - Peuples et Continents
	Germany —	Available through major booksellers with good foreign travel sections
	GB/Ireland —	Available through all booksellers with good foreign travel sections
	Italy —	Libreria dell'Automobile, Milano
	Netherlands —	Nilsson & Lamm BV, Weesp
	Denmark —	Copenhagen - Arnold Busck, G.E.C. Gad, Boghallen, G.E.C. Gad
	Finland —	Helsinki — Akateeminen Kirjakauppa
	Norway —	Oslo - Arne Gimnes/J.G. Tanum
	Sweden —	Stockholm/Esselte, Akademi Bokhandel, Fritzes, Hedengrens Gothenburg/Gumperts, Esselte Lund/Gleerupska
	Switzerland —	Basel/Bider: Berne/Atlas; Geneve/Artou; Lausanne/Artou: Zurich/Travel Bookshop

Contents

Part 1: Planning Your Holiday

1 About the Canary Islands 9
The charm of the Canaries 9 — Their situation 10 Climate 11 — When to go 13 — Tourist information 13 — Spanish Tourist Offices 14 — Arrival by air 15 — Arrival by sea (from Cadiz) 16 — Ports in the Canary Islands 19 — Inter-island ferry services 20 — Cruises 21 — Arrival by yacht 21

2 Where to stay 23
The range of accommodation 24 — Camping 26 — Travel agents' services 29 — Package holidays 30 — Time share 30 — Property and real estate agents 31

3 Getting about in the Canaries 33
Driving in Spain and the Canary Islands 33 — Taxis 35 — Buses 36 — Excursions 36

4 Food and drink 39
Buying food 39 — Local dishes 40 — Drinks 42 — Bars and restaurants 43

5 Practical information for visitors 45
British Consul 45 — Budgeting for your holiday 45 — Chemists 46 — Church services 46 — Clothes 46 — Communications 47 — Dentists 50 — Doctors 50 — Duty free allowances 51 — Electricity, radio and television 51 — Fire precautions 51 — Hairdressing 52 — Health 52 — Laundry and dry cleaning 53 — Medical services 53 — Money and banks 53 — Newspapers and books 54 — Opticians 54 — Police 54 — Problems and complaints 55 — Public conveniences 55 — Taking children to the Canary Islands 55 — Time 56 — Tipping 56 — Water 57

6 The Canary Islands and the islanders 59
History of the Canary Islands 59 — The Canarian way of life 63 — Language 65 — A botanist's paradise 65 — Wildlife 68 — Agriculture 70 — Fishing industry 72 — National holidays 72 — Fiestas and festivals 73 — Canary music and dancing 74 — Handicrafts 75

Part 2: Lanzarote

7 Introducing Lanzarote 79
Fire island 79 — History 81 — Climate 81 — Places of interest 83 — Beaches 85 — Accommodation 88 — Getting about 90 — Excursions 93

8 Restaurants, nightlife and leisure activities 97
Restaurants 97 — Nightlife 101 — Shopping 103 — Art galleries and museums 104 — Concerts 105 — Sports 106

9 Arrecife 111
The capital city 111 — **City tour 1:** Castillo de San Gabriel, Market, Iglesia de San Ginés, León y Castillo, Craft Market, Las Buganvillas, Playa Reducto 112 — **City tour 2:** Castillo de San José 114

10 Touring Lanzarote 117
Island tour 1: Arrecife, Aeropuerto de Lanzarote, Playa de los Pocillos, Puerto del Carmen 117 — **Island tour 2:** Puerto del Carmen, Mácher, Puerto Calero, Playa Quemada, Uga, Yaiza, Salinas de Janubio, Los Hervideros, El Golfo 120 — **Island tour 3:** Salinas de Janubio, Fémes, Playa Blanca, Papagayo 126 — **Island tour 4:** Timanfaya National Park 129 — **Island tour 5:** Timanfaya, Mancha Blanca, Tinajo, La Santa, Tiagua, Muñique, Sóo, Tao, Mozaga, San Bartolomé, Zonzamaz Ruins, Costa Teguise 134 — **Island tour 6:** Costa Teguise, Tahíce, Teguise, La Caleta de Famara, Los Valles, Haría, Mirador del Río 138 — **Island tour 7:** Mirador del Río, Orzola, Cuevas de los Verdes, Jameos del Agua, Arrieta, Mala, Guatiza, Costa Teguise 143

Part 3: Fuerteventura

11 Introducing Fuerteventura 149
Island of Solitude 149 — History of Fuerteventura 150 — Climate 152 — Places of special interest 153 — Beaches 154 — Accommodation 156 — Getting about 158 — Excursions 161

12 Restaurants, nightlife and leisure activities 163
Restaurants 163 — Nightlife 164 — Shopping 165 — Sports 167

13 Puerto del Rosario 171
The capital city 171 — **City tour:** León y Castillo, Iglesia de la Virgen del Rosario, Market, Handicraft shop, La Pluma Roja 172

14 Touring Fuerteventura 175
Island tour 1: Puerto del Rosario, Las Dunas, Corralejo, Isla de Los Lobos 175 — **Island tour 2:** Corralejo, Lajares, El Cotillo, La Oliva, Puertito de los Molinos, Tetir, Puerto del Rosario 179 — **Island tour 3:** Puerto del Rosario, Casillas del Angel, La Ampuyenta, La Antigua, Tuinje, Pájara, Ajuy, Puerto de la Peña, Betancuria, Llanos de la Concepción, Puerto del Rosario 183 — **Island tour 4:** Puerto del Rosario, Aeropuerto Estancas, Caleta de Fuste, Pozo Negro, Las Playitas, Gran Tarajal 191 — **Island tour 5:** Gran Tarajal, Tarajalejo, Playa de la Pared, Costa Calma, Playa Jandía, Morro Jable, Cofete, Punta de Jandía 195

Finale 202

Appendices

A Spanish-English vocabulary 203
B Wind force: the Beaufort Scale 206
C Useful conversion tables 208
D Bibliography 212

Index 213

Foreword

'Across the seas we beheld Seven Islands, each with its own special delight'

This guide has been written with the object of enlightening the reader as to the many delights of the golden Canary Islands. The Canaries consist of seven main islands which lie in the Atlantic, some seventy miles (112 km) west of North Africa. They are divided into Western and Eastern Provinces.

With a wonderful climate all the year, sandy beaches, exotic landscapes, a range of accommodation to suit all tastes, and shops stocked with a wide selection of low priced goods, the Canary Islands are a paradise for the holidaymaker.

Details are given explaining how to get there, costs, where and when to travel, with plenty of information about accommodation, attactions and local life. Facts and information are as accurate as possible at the time of going to press. The exchange rate quoted, 194 pesetas to £1, was average at the time the book was written. These are free trade islands and you get good value for your money as many items are subject only to local taxes.

This Guide describes Lanzarote and Fuerteventura in the Eastern Canary Islands. A sister volume is a guide about Gran Canaria. The Western Canary Islands, Tenerife, La Gomera, La Palma and El Hierro are published in a separate volume.

Most of all we hope that these books will help you to know, visit and enjoy the Canary Islands, as we have done.

ONE

About the Canary Islands

The charm of the Canaries

One of the delights of the Canary Islands is the knowledge that you will be able to enjoy a climate that is warm and sunny, yet remains fresh and spring-like all the year.

Seven large islands and six small islets form the Canary archipelago in the Atlantic Ocean, 112 km west of North Africa on a line with the Bahamas and 480 km north of the Tropics. These are happy peaceful islands, whose people welcome visitors with a natural friendliness.

The Canary Islands are easily accessible by air and sea, and there is accommodation to suit every taste and pocket, from top class hotel, modern apartment, and pretty villa to simple guesthouse. Constant sun shines from clear blue skies over landscapes that are so diverse that the islands have been described as a 'continent in miniature'. There is a wonderful choice of pastimes and pleasures. Sunbathing, swimming and a variety of sports can be enjoyed daily. The main tourist resorts offer a wide range of entertainments, including a lively night life, with plenty of bars and restaurants, music and dancing.

The Canaries are where you can enjoy breakfast on a sunlit terrace, take a drive into the mountains amid green forests of sweetly perfumed pine and heather, walk amongst sand dunes or ride a camel. You can lunch at a little fishing village while watching fishermen mending their nets; laze the afternoon away on a golden beach, then go shopping in an Arab Souk or visit a needlework school. In the evening you can stroll along the *plazas* with the Canarians, and have a cool drink on a colourful patio while the sun goes down over calm waters; dine by moonlight at a table under the stars, watch folk dancing, and go on to a disco or night club.

The Canary Islands have so much to offer the visitor; with their vast mountains, dense forests, green valleys, black volcanic landscapes and golden beaches, they must surely be the most delightful of all holiday destinations.

Of recent years, Lanzarote and Fuerteventura have had an upsurge in the number of British visitors. This is mainly because they are quieter islands and the development of the tourist resorts is more controlled than in Tenerife and Gran Canaria.

Their situation

The Canary Islands are an archipelago of seven major islands, Tenerife, Gomera, La Palma, El Hierro, Gran Canaria, Lanzarote and Fuerteventura, and six small islets, Isla de los Lobos, Isla Graçiosa, Isla de Montana Clara, Isla de Alegranza, Roque del Oeste and Roque del Este. The archipelago, which is sone 7500 sq. km. in area, is situated in the Atlantic Ocean 112 kms west of Morocco and 1120 kms south of Spain, at a latitude of 28°, south of the islands of Madeira. The Tropic of Cancer lies 480 km to the south. Lanzarote is just 90 kms west of the coast of Africa, being the nearest of the Canary Islands to that continent. Fuerteventura lies south east of Lanzarote and the distance between the south of Lanzarote and the north of Fuerteventura is approximately 16 kms.

The appearance of the Canary Islands indicates that they were formed by a number of violent volcanic eruptions many years ago so there is much evidence of volcanic cones and lava. The highest point of eruption was Mount Teide, in Tenerife.

Generally speaking the five most westerly islands, Gran Canaria, Tenerife, La Palma, Gomera and El Hierro are more mountainous and green. Lanzarote and Fuerteventura, being dry desert, are immensely interesting and similar to parts of North Africa. The islands tend to have steep coastal cliffs in the north while the southern coasts are more level. Except for Lanzarote all have central high mountains. Typical island features are rocky mountains, thick forests, deeply wooded ravines, fertile plains, volcanic wasteland and stretches of sand dunes. The best beaches are mainly on the east and south coasts. Some are pure golden or white, others are volcanic black sand.

The five small islets off the north of Lanzarote, are La Graciosa, Alegranza, Montana Clara, Roque del Oeste and Roque del Este. The islet of Graciosa is 42 sq kms in area and can be clearly seen from Lanzarote, just a kilometre away. The population of 800 reside mainly at Caleta del Sebo, living by fishing and visits from tourists. The village has only recently got electricity. Lovely golden beaches have been earmarked for future development. The other four islets are uninhabited, except for sea birds.

Between Lanzarote and Fuerteventura is the islet of Los Lobos, just 6.5 sq kms. The only village is El Puertito, where the fishermen supplement their income from the holidaymakers who visit from Corralejo, the port in the north of Fuerteventura. Day trips can be made only when the sea is calm. The channel between Fuerteventura and Los Lobos, called La Bocaina, is noted for its strong currents and huge Atlantic rollers. It is also a plentiful fishing ground.

Climate

The Canary Islands are warm and fresh with spring-like weather. The mean temperature varies between 25°C and 18°C, with many days of brilliant sunshine; midday temperatures can reach 32°C, or more. The average sea temperature in winter is 18°C and in summer 22°C, making all year round swimming possible.

The small amount of rain falls mainly in the north of the islands, where it is more green with a humidity of between 60% and 69%. The rainfall is governed by the mountains on each island and varies accordingly. Tenerife and Gran Canaria have more rainfall than Lanzarote and Fuerteventura. Rain is heaviest between November and February — June, July and August being the driest months.

Winds are predominantly northwesterly occasionally veering to easterly when they bring hot air and dusty sand from North Africa. The latter wind is called the *sirocco* and usually lasts three to four days. Because of the light breezes that blow most days, the climate is invigorating and gives a sense of well being.

And because of the mountains and the fact that the islands are small land masses, there can be considerable change in the weather on the same day. The north can be cloudy while the south remains sunny. There is a saying that somewhere on every island there is sunshine every day.

The sun sinks quickly in these latitudes giving short evenings, so often spectacular sunsets are seen. The nights can be very clear and conducive to star gazing. Because of the clear air an Astro-Physical Observatory has been built on the island of La Palma.

Sufferers from bronchitis, influenza and asthma find much relief when staying in the Canary Islands, especially during the winter months. However those suffering from respiratory ailments should not settle in the city of Las Palmas, Gran Canaria, because of the acknowledged pollution problem caused by traffic congestion, dust

Climatic Chart

Average temperature	Jan	Feb	Mar	Apr	May	Jun	Jul	Aug	Sep	Oct	Nov	Dec	Yearly
°C	17.8	17.9	18.5	19.3	20.4	22.0	23.6	24.2	24.0	23.5	21.5	18.8	21.7
°F	64.0	64.2	65.3	66.7	68.7	71.6	74.4	75.5	75.2	74.3	70.7	65.8	71
Humidity%	67	67	66	64	63	63	59	60	65	68	69	67	65
Cloudy days	2	1	0	0	1	0	0	0	0	0	1	2	7
Clear days	6	6	6	8	7	8	11	12	9	6	3	4	86
Sunny days	18	16	20	18	18	16	13	12	17	18	17	16	199
Rainy days	7.5	6	4.9	4	2	1	1	1	2	6	10	9	54

from building projects and the occasional *sirocco* dust storm from the Sahara Desert.

Thus one of the biggest incentives to visit the Canary Islands is its predictable climate. With so little variation during the year and from one year to another, visitors can be assured of sunshine practically every day. Even if there is cloud, it will not be cold. The few rainy days do not last for long, then the sun shines again.

When to go

The Canary Islands are ideal for all-the-year-round holidays. During the summer months a high proportion of Spanish nationals visit the islands. During the period October to May, the majority of visitors come from the cooler climates of Germany, Scandinavia, Holland and France. Many local shop keepers and restaurant owners take their holidays during the month of June, which (they say) can be a slack month. It is also the cheapest travel period for package tours. The peak period is from November to February when a high percentage of the accommodation is booked in advance; this is the time of the year when most tourists from the UK arrive. Christmas to New Year is the most expensive period but good value.

Because of the constant demand in the most popular tourist areas of Puerto de la Cruz in Tenerife, Playa del Inglés in Gran Canaria and Puerto del Carmen in Lanzarote, it is advisable to plan one's visit in advance, especially over the Christmas period.

Some hotels and apartments have tariff variations as follows:

Low season — 1 May to 30 June Mid season — 1 July to 31 October
High season — 1 November to 30 April

Tourist information

Visitors to the Canary Islands require a valid passport, which must be stamped by the Spanish Immigration Authority on entry, with arrival date. It is your responsibility to see this done, otherwise your entry is illegal. You do not need a visa for a stay of up to 90 days, but after this it may be necessary. Information can be obtained from: **The Spanish Consulate,** 20 Draycott Place, London SW3. Tel: 071 581 5921.

Up to date tourist information can be obtained from **The Spanish**

National Tourist Office, 57/58 St James's Street, London SW1 Tel: 071 499 0901.

Vaccinations are not normally needed for the Canary Islands. Only in the case of an epidemic would they be required.

Visitors are allowed to bring in any amount of foreign currency in notes or travellers cheques and up to 150,000 pesetas. You may take out 100,000 pesetas and foreign currency equivalent to 500,000 pesetas (£2,577).

Spanish Tourist Offices

The Spanish Tourist Industry is organised through the Secretaria de Estado, part of the Ministerio de Transportes, Turismo y Comunicaciones and funded by the State. The Secretaria has a delegation in the capital of each province and public information offices are also there.

Oficinas Municipales de Turismo are situated in towns and villages of particular tourist interest and are there to provide information, free of charge. It is recommended that use be made of these tourist offices in the Canary Islands; they can supply lists of accommodation, island and town maps, and literature often with good pictures. Although in some offices the staff may have only a limited knowledge of English, much effort is made to assist tourists. They can be found in:

Western Province

Tenerife	Palacio Insular, Santa Cruz de Tenerife. Tel: 24 22 27.
La Palma	Calle O'Daly, Santa Cruz de la Palma.
Gomera	Ayuntamiento, General Franco 20, San Sebastián.
El Hierro	Cabildo Insular del Hierro, Valverde.

Eastern Province

Gran Canaria	Parque Santa Catalina, Las Palmas. Tel: 26 46 23.
Lanzarote	Parque Municipale, Arrecife. (Open 0900 to 1300 and 1730 to 1900 hrs)
Fuerteventura	Ministerio de Trabajo, Avenida General Franco, Puerto del Rosario. (Open 0830 to 1500 hrs)

Arrival by air

Of the seven islands, La Gomera is the only one that does not have an airport but there is a project to build one near Santiago in the south of the island. However there are frequent ferries from Los Cristianos in the south of Tenerife to San Sebastián de la Gomera.

The airports of the Canaries

Tenerife	— Aeropuerto Los Rodeos (Inter Island)
	— Aeropuerto Reina Sofia (International)
Gran Canaria	— Aeropuerto de Gando
Fuerteventura	— Aeropuerto Los Estancas (Puerto del Rosario)
Lanzarote	— Aeropuerto de Lanzarote (Arrecife)
El Hierro	— Aeropuerto del Hierro (Valverde)
La Palma	— Aeropuerto de la Palma

The airport at El Hierro is virtually a landing strip, but it is of good size and sufficient for return flights each day between Tenerife and El Hierro. On all the other islands the airports are modern and efficient and well able to cope with the traffic, which sometimes is very heavy.

The system for handling passengers and their luggage is the same as for all international airports and the Spanish have no wish to slow the flow of tourists. It is necessary only to have your passport stamped with the date of entry. The airports are well served with taxis and buses. Booking arrangements for hotels, apartments and car rental at Tenerife, Gran Canaria and Lanzarote can be made from the airport. At present the airport at Fuerteventura does not have the facility for booking accommodation. You would need to seek the assistance of a taxi driver or travel agent *(viaje)*.

The airport at Lanzarote deserves a special mention. It was designed by the local born César Manrique. The interior decor is green and white, the ceiling is lined with green and white canvas. There is green upholstered seating and many potted palms and ferns. It resembles the lounge of a luxury hotel or a tent belonging to a rich sultan!

Further airport information is given in the chapters dealing with individual islands.

Air services

Scheduled air services from London Heathrow and Gatwick direct to the Canary Islands, including Lanzarote and Fuerteventura, are provided by Iberia (Spanish) and Britannia Airways. The return fare is between £129 and £259, with weekly and seasonal variations. Iberia also fly from London Heathrow to the Canaries via Madrid or Seville.

There are several charter flights used by package operators, which fly direct between the UK and the Canary Islands. Seats on these aircraft are sometimes available, without accommodation. Travel agents are able to supply details. Prices vary according to the season but can be lower than those of Iberia. The flight time between London/Gatwick and Gran Canaria/Las Palmas is 4 hours, and to Lanzarote/Arrecife or Fuerteventura/Los Estancas is 3¾ hours.

Inter island flight times

Gando Airport Las Palmas (Gran Canaria)	to Reina Sophia/Los Rodeos (Tenerife)	— 35 mins
	to Los Estancas (Fuerteventura)	— 30 mins
	to La Palma (La Palma)	— 40 mins
	to Arrecife (Lanzarote)	— 35 mins

Costs are: Las Palmas to Lanzarote or Fuerteventura, single, 4500 pesetas (£23); between Lanzarote and Fuerteventura, single, 1800 pesetas (£9.27).

Arrival by sea (from Cadiz)

The only car and passenger service operating from Spain to the Canary Islands is from Cadiz (southern Spain) to Tenerife, Gran Canaria and Lanzarote, and it is operated by the Trasmediterranea Shipping Company. It is not possible to go directly to the other islands, though there are ferries to La Palma, El Hierro and Gomera from Tenerife, and to Lanzarote and Fuerteventura from Gran Canaria. But first you have to get to Cadiz . . .

By rail to Cadiz

Rail tickets for travel from UK to Cadiz, Spain, can be obtained from: **British Rail Continental Ltd,** Ticket and Information Office, P.O. Box No. 29, London SW1V 1JX. Tel: 071 834 2345 or through a travel agent. There are no Spanish Railway Agents in U.K. Example of fare: London to Cadiz, 2nd class return — £175.

The windmills of Lanzarote are now a picturesque feature but in the past they were important for grinding corn.

By road to Cadiz

The most direct way is to cross from Plymouth (Devon) to Santander in northern Spain and then drive south to Cadiz (see Driving in Spain — p. 00). Brittany Ferries operate a regular car and passenger ferry (from Millbay Docks, Plymouth) throughout the year. The crossing takes twenty-four hours in fully stabilised ships. Driving into the car deck is a simple operation. The ships are comfortable with air-conditioned de luxe, two- and four-berth cabins, some with showers and toilets. There are wide promenade and sun decks, lounges with bars and dance floor, restaurant, duty free shop, cinema, games and children's room.

Arriving in Santander, there are many routes across Spain, the most direct being via Burgos, Madrid, Cordoba and Sevilla to Cadiz. Distance on this route is 1165 km.

Alternatively, cross to France by using any of the Channel ports and travel overland to Spain, thence down to Cadiz in the south. However, during the winter months the mountain passes in northern Spain and Andorra can be closed by snow. An alternative route is to drive down to the French Mediterranean and continue along the east coast line of Spain to reach Cadiz.

Yet another variation is to reach Spain and drive along the north east coast, then down the western coast into Portugal and along the Algarve to Spain and Cadiz. The latter route, though much longer, gives a very scenic drive.

Example of Brittany Ferries cross channel costs (which vary with type of accommodation and length of vehicle) for car and two persons, single, mid season: Plymouth to Santander — £250; Plymouth to Roscoff — £95; Portsmouth to St Malo — £126; Portsmouth to Caen — £87 (day).

Brittany Ferries Millbay Docks, Plymouth, PQ7 8RU. Tel: 0752 21321

P. & O. Ferries, Freepost, Southampton, SO9 1BG.

Sealink Travel Ltd, PO Box 29, Victoria Station, London SW1V 1JX. Tel: 071 834 8122.

The ferry from Cadiz

During the winter months there is a Saturday ferry departure from Cadiz in southern Spain to the Canary Islands. During the summer months (16 Jun-12 Sep) there are departures on Tuesday, Thursday and Saturday. All sailings call at Santa Cruz (Tenerife), Las Plamas (Gran Canaria) and Arrecife (Lanzarote) and return to Cadiz in the reverse order, leaving from Arrecife.

The journey takes about two days. This is the only ferry service operating from the Spanish mainland to the Canaries and it is advisable to book well in advance.

There are two ferry ships operating the service at present, the 'J.J. Sister' and the 'Manuel Soto'. They are similar, of about 10,000 tons each carrying 743 passengers and 250 vehicles. Described as floating hotels, they have a swimming pool, à la carte restaurant, self-service cafeteria, bars, sport facilities, reading room, dance floor, cinema, television, shop, hairdresser, children's playroom and lifts. There is First and Tourist Class, with two, three and four berth cabin accommodation. Trasmediterranea are planning to add another ship to their service between Cadiz and the Canaries. The 'Bolero', presently owned by Fred Olsen, can carry 1600 passengers, 400 vehicles and has 748 cabins.

The Trasmediterranea ferry ships operating between the islands are smaller but services are adequate considering that the voyages are of shorter duration, about seven hours and usually overnight. First and Tourist Class accommodation is provided. All Trasmediterranea ferries have vehicle space, which is drive-on/drive-off. On occasions it may be necessary to reverse on to the car deck.

The UK agent for Trasmediterranea is: **Melia Travel** 12 Dover Street, London W1. Tel: 071 499 6731. Reservations can also be made in Spain through travel agents. Trasmediterranea have offices in a number of towns in Spain.

In Cadiz: Avenida de Carranza, 26. Tel: 28 43 50. Telex 76028.

In Madrid: (Head Office) Plaza Manuel Gomez Moreno. Tel: 456 00 07. Telex 27731.

In Las Palmas: Aucona, Muelle Santa Catalina. Tel: 26 00 70.

In Santa Cruz de Tenerife: Marina 59. Tel: 28 78 50.

Ports in the Canary Islands

The locations of ports in the Canary Islands where ships arrive and depart are:

Lanzarote Arrecife; Playa Blanca

Fuerteventura Puerto del Rosario; Corralejo; Morro Jable; Gran Tarajal

Gran Canaria Las Palmas de Gran Canaria

Tenerife Santa Cruz de Tenerife; Los Cristianos

La Palma Santa Cruz de la Palma

Gomera San Sebastian de Gomera

El Hierro Puerto de la Estaca

Inter island ferry services

The **Trasmediterranea Shipping Company** operates an inter island vehicle and passenger service that connects all seven islands. There is a daily service between Tenerife and Gran Canaria. The other islands of Lanzarote, Fuerteventura, Gomera, Hierro and La Palma are visited at least twice a week.

The inter island ferries usually provide pleasant sea crossings, despite the fact that the ships are old. In winter, owing to Atlantic squalls, the sea can be rough. There are cabins or armchairs *(butacas),* bar, cafeteria and shop available. Sailings are usually overnight.

The single fare for two persons and car between Las Palmas (Gran Canaria) and Lanzarote or Fuerteventura is about 20,000 pesetas (£103). Reservations can be made at most travel agents. Trasmediterranea have offices at all the ports.

In addition to the vehicle and passenger ferry, Trasmediterranea operate Jetfoils between:

- Santa Cruz de Tenerife and Las Palmas (Gran Canaria) four times daily, taking 80 minutes, single fare 4220 pesetas (£21.75).
- Santa Cruz de Tenerife and Morro Jable (Fuerteventura) once a day, taking 2 hours, single fare, 6080 pesetas (£31.34).
- Las Palmas (Gran Canaria) and Morro Jable (Fuerteventura) once a day, taking 90 minutes.
- Playa Blanca (Lanzarote) and Corralejo (Fuerteventura) four times daily, taking 20 minutes, single fare 1950 pesetas (£10).
- Playa Blanca (Lanzarote) and Puerto del Rosario (Fuerteventura) taking 60 minutes, single fare 2950 pesetas (£15.20).
- Puerto del Rosario and Corralejo (Fuerteventura) taking 40 minutes, single fare 1000 pesetas (£2).

The Alisur vehicle and passenger ferry

The Alisur Ferry Company provides six services daily between Corralejo (Fuerteventura) and Playa Blanca (Lanzarote), taking 45 minutes. It is a small open-decked, vessel. Single fare, 1500 pesetas (£7.73); vehicle and two passengers, 5500 pesetas (£28).

Ferry Betancuria

The Ferry Betancuria is a modern vehicle and passenger ferry providing a thrice daily service between Corralejo and Playa Blanca, taking 35 minutes to make the crossing. Single fare, 2900 pesetas (£14.94); vehicle and two passengers, 6900 pesetas (£35.56).

Cruises

The following companies operate inclusive luxury liner cruises to the Canary Islands:
Fred Olsen Line, 11 Conduit Street, London. Tel: 071 409 2019.
P & O 'Princess' and 'Canberra' Cruises, Beaufort House, St Botolph Street, London EC3. Tel: 071 377 2551.
Costa Cruises, Costa Line, 16 Maddox Street, London.
CTC Lines, 1 Lower Regent Street, London W1. Tel: 071 930 5833
Cunard, 8 Berkeley Street, London. Tel: 071 491 3930.
Europe Cruise Line, Sally Holidays, 81 Piccadilly, London. Tel: 071 355 2266.

Cruise ships call at Santa Cruz de Tenerife, Las Palmas de Gran Canaria and Arrecife, Lanzarote.

Arrival by yacht

For those who have the necessary skills and a suitable yacht, it is possible to reach the Canary Islands, though it is well to realise they are in the Atlantic Ocean, not the Mediterranean. For up to date details write to:
National Assembly of Yacht Captains, Muelle España, Zona Deportiva, Barcelona, Spain; or
The Spanish Sailing Federation, Juan Vigon 23, Madrid, Spain.

Yacht and boat facilities

The Canary Islands are ideally situated for yachts and motor vessels, having many suitable marinas and moorings, natural sheltered bays and harbours. Many boats moor there for the winter season, some waiting, as Christopher Colombus did, for the trade winds to take them to the West Indies. There are yacht marinas

- **In Tenerife:** Real Club Náutico, Carretera de San Andres, Santa Cruz de Tenerife. Tel: 27 37 00.
- **In Gran Canaria:** Real Club Náutico, Leon y Castillo, Las Palmas. Tel: 23 45 66.
- **In Lanzarote:** Casino Club Náutico, Calle Blas Cabrera Felipe, Arrecife (Private); Urbanisation y Puerto Deportivo, Puerto Calero. Tel: 82 55 94; Yacht Marina, Playa Blanca. (Facilities for

A modern marina at Puerto Naos in Arrecife harbour gives calm moorings close to the island's capital.

yachts at Puerto Naos, Arrecife are not yet completed.)

- **In Fuerteventura:** Yacht Marina, Caleta de Fuste. (Facilities at Corralejo and Morro Jable are not yet completed.)
- **In La Palma:** New Royal Yacht Club, General Mola 6, Santa Cruz de la Palma, Tel: 41 11 84.
- **In La Gomera:** Yacht Club, Calle del Conde, San Sebastián de la Gomera. Tel: 87 10 53.

TWO

Where to stay

Accommodation in the Canaries ranges from luxury hotels to simple guesthouses and camping. In Tenerife and Gran Canaria the choice is vast. Lanzarote has increased the number of beds available to tourists recently, but the development is being strictly controlled to suit the island's amenities. Fuerteventura has a new building programme in the south, but at the moment accommodation is not plentiful. La Palma, La Gomera and El Hierro have little tourist accommodation, except for the *paradors* there.

An up to date list of all types of accommodation currently available can be obtained from the Tourist Offices. For Tenerife, La Palma, Gomera and El Hierro the address is:
The Tourist Office (Palacio Insular), Plaza España, Santa Cruz de Tenerife. Tel: 24 22 27. For Gran Canaria, Lanzarote and Fuerteventura: The Tourist Office, Parque Santa Catalina, Las Palmas de Gran Canaria. Tel: 26 46 23.

The cost of non-package accommodation is similar on all the islands, but in each group there is a variation of tariff according to season: high season — 1 November to 30 April; mid season — 1 July to 31 October; low season — 1 May to 30 June.

To give you an idea of charges, they range as follows (for double room without breakfast):

- Five-star hotel: 13,000 pesetas (£67) to 17,000 pesetas £87.62)
- Four-star hotel: 6000 pesetas (£30.92) to 10,000 pesetas (£51.54)
- Three-star hotel: 4000 pesetas (£20.61) to 7000 pesetas (£36)
- Two-star hotel: 2000 pesetas (£10.30)
- One-star hotel: 1500 pesetas (£7.73)
- Pension: 500 pesetas (£2.57) to 3000 pesetas (£15.46)

We wish to emphasis that prices are increasing all the time and that a tax (I.T.E.) of 4% is added to all accommodation accounts.

The range of accommodation

It is recommended that you choose accommodation that has been inspected by the Tourist Board and that you book through property or travel agents. It is unwise to seek unlisted places, especially in the cities where some proprietors may not observe security regulations nor maintain hygiene standards.

Hotels

Hotels (*Hoteles* — H) are classified from 1 to 5 stars. The rating is always displayed outside as H plus the number of stars. Hotels provide rooms and meals as required in their own restaurant. The larger hotels usually have outdoor swimming pools, tennis courts, shops and entertainment. Many have courtesy buses to take visitors to the beach. Those with three stars or more provide rooms with private bathrooms and toilets. Most have balconies often with sea views. Maid service and laundry service should be available.

The impressive-looking Arrecife Gran Hotel is one of the few high rise buildings in Lanzarote.

Hotel Apartments

Hotel Apartments (*Apartamentos Hoteles* — HA) are similar to hotels but have flats, bungalows or chalets. The star rating is shown after HA.

Resident Hotels

These hotels (*Hoteles Residencia* — HR) supply rooms but without restaurant facilities. They usually have less luxurious furnishings though often have private bathrooms and toilets. Shown as HR with star rating.

Guesthouses

Modest hotels and guesthouses (*Hostales* — HS) with star rating of one to three. They provide accommodation with or without meals. They do not have dormitories.

Pensions

Guesthouses (*Pensionés* — P) with a small number of rooms, providing full board.

Residences

These establishments (*Residencias* — R) provide accommodation with a shared bathroom. Breakfast only available.

Inns

Inns (*pousadas, tabernas*) are usually in country districts; the standard is mostly good, but can vary. It is best to view rooms before booking. They are often in beautiful surroundings with local atmosphere.

Paradors

A *parador* is the name given to hotels of the State Secretariat for Tourism (Parador Nacionales de Turismo) in Spain and the Canary Islands. Usually they are in converted historic castles, palaces, convents and monasteries and generally in a location of special scenic beauty or interest. Internal decor is of a luxurious standard, often containing antiques and works of art. They offer every comfort as well as an excellent cuisine. The restaurants are open to non-residents. Sometimes *paradors* can be more expensive than equivalent hotels but they provide a unique tourist experience. It is advisable to book in advance.

The Spanish Tourist Office publishes an informative brochure called *Paradores,* which is given free on request. In the Eastern

Canaries there are *paradors* in:
Fuerteventura — Parador Nacional de Fuerteventura: Three-star modern building overlooking Puerto del Rosario and the sea. 24 rooms, swimming pool. Tel: 85 11 50.
Gran Canaria — Parador Nacional de Tejeda: Two-star Canary style modern building. 19 bedrooms, bar restaurant open to visitors. Splendid views, high altitude. Tel: 65 80 50.
There is no Parador Nacional in Lanzarote.

Apartments

Self-catering accommodation is available on all the main islands. In the big resorts purpose-built blocks are of enormous size, having their own restaurants, public rooms, swimming pools, sports facilities, supermarket, hairdressing salon and boutique. Some have evening entertainments, such as flamenco shows and music groups.

In the apartments (*apartamentos*), basic provisions will include bed linen, towels, kitchen equipment and cooking facilities, with cutlery, crockery and glasses. The majority have balconies often with sea views. High rise blocks have lifts. Most provide maid service but in some cases only once a week.

At the reception, details will be found of local entertainment, coach excursions and car hire.

Bungalows and villas

Often built around a swimming pool, bungalows and villas are more attractive as they usually have gardens and shrubs close by. There are always restaurants, bars and supermarkets in the vicinity. Information can be obtained from travel agents.

Camping

Camping rules that apply in mainland Spain also apply in the Canary Islands. A copy of the camping regulations should be obtained by anyone intending to camp in the Canaries. This can be obtained from: **The Spanish Tourist Office** 57-58 St James's Street, London SW1A 1LD. Tel: 071 499 0901.

It is not necessary to have a Camping Carnet, but it is an advantage, particularly for those who camp outside sites, as third party insurance is included. Camping Carnets can be obtained from camping and motoring organisations such as the AA, RAC and Caravan Club, and cost approximately £2. A passport-size photo is required.

Camping on site
You will be required to present your passport at the camp site reception. Persons under the age of 16 may not be admitted unless accompanied by an adult. Silence must be respected between 2300 and 0800 hours. Fires are not permitted except in allocated places. Campers are not allowed to carry offensive weapons. Valuables may be left with the camp manager for safe keeping. Most sites have their own post boxes and supermarkets. Every reception office has an official complaints book.

Camping off site
Camping is allowed outside official camp sites provided one has the permission of the owner of the land. Camping is not allowed in the following places: on dry river beds, seasonal flooding areas; within military, industrial or tourist areas; within a radius of 150 metres from the source of a town's water supply; within urban areas or unreasonably near the roadside; within one kilometre of an official camp site.

Backpackers
Since camping is not permitted in most tourist areas campers are not welcome on some beaches. In the past, the 'hippy' type of backpacker has caused the authorities much trouble: hence the reluctance to let groups of campers forgather. However, backpackers do visit the islands, using simple hostels with the odd night camping; but care is required in conforming with the regulations.

Caravans
The terrain of the Canary Islands is not conducive to touring with a towed caravan, these can be accommodated at Camping Guantanamo, Tauro or Camping Pasito Blanco in Gran Canaria, and Camping Nauta in Tenerife. Or owners use their caravans to cross Europe, then stay at a rented villa or apartment. A few hardy caravanners may find quiet places which are suitable for a short stay, having obtained permission from the police or the owner: these sites, usually on waste ground, are few and far between.

Motorcaravans
At present there are no official camping places in Lanzarote or Fuerteventura. The authorities are aware of this and tolerate free parking on some beaches when it is not causing a public nuisance. Motorcaravan windsurf enthusiasts tend to visit Lanzarote and

A windsurfing motorcaravanner looks out to sea to assess the wind at Lanzarote's Papagayo beach in Lanzarote, where free camping is permitted.

Fuerteventura where there are Windsurfing Schools. They favour La Santa, Costa Teguise and Puerto del Carmen in Lanzarote. In Fuerteventura, Corralejo, Playa de Castillo and Jandía Playa are popular places. We have always enjoyed our motorcaravan holidays in both Lanzarote and Fuerteventura.

Certainly the most suitable way to camp in the Canary Islands is to use a motorcaravan. The diversity of scenery and regions makes travelling interesting and varied. Provided one parks with consideration to the regulations there should be few problems.

Hints for campers

One of the main requirements of all campers is water, which, in the Canary Islands, is in short supply. Therefore it is necessary to conserve and plan ahead. Most petrol filling stations will allow containers to be filled but make sure that it is drinking water (*agua potable*) or buy bottled water from a supermarket. Camping 'Gaz' is available in towns and some villages. A 907 refill costs 350 pesetas.

Further information on camping in the Canary Islands can be obtained from periodicals such as *Caravan; Camping and Walking; Motorcaravan and Motorhome Monthly; Which Motorcaravan, Motorcaravan* and *Motorcaravan World.*

Travel agents' services

There are numerous travel agents *(viajes)* in the tourist parts of the Canary Islands. Their services are varied: they may be agents for hotels, apartments, ferry and flight bookings; car hire, coach tours and currency exchange. Open from 0900 to 1300 and 1630 to 1900 hrs, Monday to Friday, 0900 to 1300 hrs on Saturday and closed on Sundays and Public Holidays.

In Lanzarote

Insular, La Penita, Puerto del Carmen. Tel: 82 59 96.
Lanzarote Travel, Gines de Castro 3, Arrecife. Tel: 81 42 54.
Tisalaya, Las Cucharas, Costa Teguise. Tel: 81 07 90.
Potogi, Punta Limones 18, Playa Blanca, Yaiza (no telephone).

In Fuerteventura

Best Island Travel, Jandía Beach Centre. Tel: 87 65 17.
Canyrama, Corralejo. Tel: 86 62 25.
Ultramar Express, by Hotel Oliva. Tel: 86 61 00.

Isla del Sol, Calle General Franco 2, Puerto del Rosario. Tel: 85 07 96.

Package holidays

There are many UK firms operating package holidays to the Canary Islands. These provide a wide choice of selection and offer good value to holidaymakers with a limited amount of time. They also enable customers to budget in advance for most of their holiday expenses.

When you book a package holiday, the price of the air fare is included, plus transport to and from your destination, unless otherwise stated. Tour operators' brochures will give details of flight arrangements, type of resort, entertainments and the star rating of the accommodation. These vary from five-star luxury hotels to modest guesthouses, self-catering apartments and villas. In some instances it is possible to visit more than one island during your holiday.

At present the islands of Tenerife and Gran Canaria have the most package tours available, with Lanzarote a very popular third choice. Fuerteventura has recently entered the tourist market and now has hotels in both the north and south.

Amongst the tour operators offering Canary Island packages are: Airways, Blue Skies, Cambrian, Carousel, Cosmos, Ellerman, Enterprise, Falcon (Windsurfing), Flair, Global, Ingram, Intersun, Lagoon Windsurf Tours, Lanzarote Villas, Lanzotic Travel, Mundi Color, Portland, Scotia, Silvair, Sovereign, Student Travel, Thomas Cook, Travel Club, Tjaereborg, Thomson Holidays, Wings, Yorkshire Travel.

Saga Holidays offer package deals for the 'over 60s', to Tenerife and Gran Canaria during 'off-peak' periods.

Time share

Time share is the ownership of a property (apartment or bungalow) for any period you care to purchase, such as a week, a month or more in a year. There is a once only purchase payment, and then an annual fee to cover management, maintenance, electricity and water. It is a modern way to own a holiday home for the purchased period and you are free to use it as you wish. For example, Las Brisas at Playa Blanca, Lanzarote has been developed by Wimpey for this purpose. The purchase cost for a one bedroom apartment could be about £3000 for one week a year. You are advised to seek qualified advice before signing any documents.

Property and real estate agents

The Canary Islands present an appealing location for purchasers to invest in property, but it is advisable to get specialist advice on the subject.

Selling apartments, bungalows and villas, the administration of properties, letting, legal advice, repairs, technical services and insurance, are all transactions carried out by real estate companies in the Canary Islands, and most of the firms employ multi-lingual staff, trained to assist clients.

'Time sharing' is on the increase and firms like Wimpey have recently entered the market. *Urbanizaciónes,* as property developments are called, tend to group in nationalities in particular areas. For instance, Scandinavians seem not to mix a great deal with Germans.

The British appear to favour Puerto de la Cruz and Playa de las Americas in Tenerife. Gran Canaria has British residents in the Tafira district of Las Palmas, in Playa del Inglés and Puerto Rico. A big proportion of British residents like Lanzarote where English is well understood. In Fuerteventura the British favour buying property in the north at Corralejo. Real estate companies and agents in Lanzarote where English is spoken are:

Lanzarote Villas, 37 East Street, Horsham, Sussex, UK Tel: 51304.

Lindes Estates, Carretera 79, Tias, Tel: 51 22 05 06. Fax 51 22 06. English speaking architect, professional assistance with legal services.

Cristin Bethencourt, Calle Riego 5, Arrecife.

Fun for all the family at the Oliva Beach Hotel near Corralejo, Fuerteventura, where swimming can be in the pool or sea.

THREE

Getting about in the Canaries

There are no trains in the Canary Islands so you have to get about by road. Fortunately the main roads and motorways are good, and *autopistas* (motorways) are free of tolls. Traffic is only heavy in cities and towns but the driving is well disciplined. However roads in the country are sometimes little more than rough tracks across desert land and progress can be slow.

A good map of the Canary Islands is therefore essential. Recommended is the series published by Firestone Hispania available in the Canary Islands from petrol filling stations and bookshops. In Great Britain and Ireland they can be obtained from bookshops with a strong foreign map section or direct, by post, from the agent, Roger Lascelles, 47 York Road, Brentford, Middlesex, TW8 0QP. Tel: 081-847 0935. The map references are: T-32 Canary Islands; E-50 Tenerife; E-51 Gran Canaria.

Driving in Spain and the Canary Islands

If you are taking a car to the Canary Islands, driving through Spain and taking the car ferry from Cadiz to either Tenerife or Gran Canaria, you will require the following:

1. Driving Licence
2. International Driving Permit
3. Green Card Insurance (your insurance company issues this)
4. Bail Bond (from AA, RAC or insurance company — this is an indemnity if you are involved in an accident)
5. Vehicle Registration Document
6. Passport
7. A spare set of light bulbs (Spanish law requirement)
8. A red triangle, for warning of breakdown obstruction
9. Means of changing direction of headlight dip
10. GB sticker.

Up to date information and advice on this subject is best obtained from the AA, RAC or the Spanish Tourist Office. However, the following points are worthy of note:

- Drive on the right-hand side of the road.
- Sound your horn when overtaking.
- Stop for pedestrians on crossings.
- Wear seatbelts.
- Sidelights only required in built up areas.
- Do not cross the single white line, it is equivalent to the double white line in the UK.
- Observe the no overtaking signs, and speed limits.
- Give way to traffic coming from the right, particularly at roundabouts.

Note that traffic offences are fined on the spot — carry at least 10,000 pesetas.

Road signs

Most road signs are international. One important traffic control is the *cambio de sentido* (change direction), generally controlled by traffic lights, which prevents vehicles turning across oncoming traffic or from doing a U-turn. Here are some translations:

Aduana customs post
Aparcamiento parking
Atencíon caution
Blandones soft verges
Cedo el Paso give way
Despacio slow
Desvio diversion
Derecha right
Escuela school
Estacionamiento prohibido no parking
Izquierda left
Obras workmen
Pare stop
Peligro danger
Peligroso dangerous
Paso prohibido No thoroughfare
Peatones pedestrians
Salidas exit

Petrol filling stations

In the Canary Islands some petrol filling stations are closed all day on Sundays and public holidays. They do not provide car repair services; this is a separate service, *taller mechanico.* Good toilets and drinking water can be found at filling stations. Autoshops sell spares and sweets. Car wash services are similar to those in the UK.

At the time of writing petrol is 58 pesetas (30p) per litre. It comes in three grades: Extra — 98 octane, Super — 96 octane, Normal — 92 octane. Do not confuse petrol *(gasolina)* with diesel *(gasoil).*

Car servicing and repairs

There are plenty of places for servicing and repairing cars. The cities of Tenerife and Gran Canaria have agents for most well-known British and foreign cars. There could be some delay in obtaining a particular spare part required from abroad.

In country places a small workshop (*taller mechanico*), which deals with local vehicles, will assist. The standard is good and repairs are promptly effected. Costs are usually more reasonable than in the UK. Facilities for tyre fitting, battery charging and car washing are available.

Car hire (self drive)

Car hire agencies in the Canary Islands include international names like Hertz and Avis, Organización Canaria Coches Aquiler (abbreviation OCCA) and local firms. Prices vary, so it is worth shopping around if you are in a large resort. Clients pay for petrol.

Types of car range from a luxury Mercedes to a safari jeep. Motorcycles, scooters and bicycles can also be rented. (Crash helmets have to be worn on motorcycles.)

In some instances the minimum age for drivers is 21. Passport, driving licence and a deposit of about 8000 pesetas (£41) are required. Confirm that vehicle insurance is included in the hire cost — this is usually about 500 pesetas (£2.57) per day and personal insurance 250 pesetas (£1.28) per day. It is advisable to book in advance.

There is an on-the-spot fine for failing to use seat belts and for other offences, costing up to 10,000 pesetas (£50). There is a 10% reduction if you pay immediately. Maximum speed in towns and villages is 40 kph, elsewhere 100 kph. Police patrol on motor cycles especially on the Carretera General (main road).

Taxis

Taxis are a pleasure to use on the Canary Islands and give a good but not always cheap service. Generally they are large Mercedes and kept very clean by their Canarian drivers. You may have to listen to taped Canarian music and some drivers do not allow smoking. At night most display a green light as being available for hire, also there is a sign indicating 'free' (*libre*). Taxis in the larger towns have meters and the drivers are very good at giving change, though they expect a tip (*propina*) of about ten per cent.

For those taxis that do not have meters, or if you wish to go beyond the city or town limits, it is necessary to arrange the price beforehand. Misunderstandings usually occur because of lack of communication. Some drivers will write down the price and place, which is helpful. Baggage may require a surcharge.

Buses

Both Lanzarote and Fuerteventura have an adequate bus service. Bus stops are marked, sometimes by *parada* (stopping place). You always enter a bus from the front and buy your ticket from the conductor or driver; only single journey (*ida*) tickets are issued. Remember to retain your ticket as inspectors cover all routes. Canary bus queues are usually orderly and line up facing the direction in which the bus will travel. For long distances there are fast buses having limited stops, sometimes marked *Expres* or *Directo*. Buses run every day including Public Holidays. Timetables can be obtained from Tourist Offices and some bus terminals. Further information is given in the sections describing individual islands.

Vehicles range from comfortable long distance coaches to ancient bone-shakers. The Canarians call their buses *guaguas* (pronounced 'wah wah') but *autobus* is generally understood. (See also Chapters 7 and 11.)

Excursions

There is no doubt that one of the easiest ways of enjoying the sights of the Canary Islands is to take a coach tour or sea cruise. Both Lanzarote and Fuerteventura offer these facilities. Half day, whole day and evening excursions are well advertised in hotels, apartments, travel agents and local papers. When on a package holiday your tour representative is sure to describe what can be seen and will be glad to make your reservation. Should you be an

A view of the Timanfaya National Park, where the volcanic landscape is full of weird moonlike shapes and colourful lava. 600,000 people visit this park each year.

independent traveller you can still join these tours, assuming there is a vacant seat.

Make sure that you book an excursion that has an English-speaking guide and check whether the cost includes a meal. Remember to take your sunglasses, camera, cardigan or pullover. Possibly flat shoes and a towel if it includes visiting a beach or a boat trip. Most days it is sensible to take a sunhat; even when it is not bright the sun's rays can filter through the clouds.

Your tour is likely to stop at an *artesanía* (souvenir shop) so some extra cash may be required, also for snacks and cold drinks en route. If you have young children some bottled water and sweets will be appreciated.

As well as coach and sea excursions, air tours can be enjoyed from both Lanzarote and Fuerteventura. You can visit the other Canary Islands on a day trip, or it might involve a night stop. Further details can be found on pages 93 and 161.

FOUR

Food and drink

Buying food

The Canary Islands, because of their free ports, have a great variety of food and drink. The tourist areas, especially, are full of exotic foodstuffs from all over the world.

Prices of imported foods from Spain tend to be higher than on the mainland. Most other food prices are comparable with, if not cheaper than, Europe. Of course, if you buy a tin of baked beans with an English brand name, then it will be more expensive than a similar product bearing a Canarian or Spanish brand name.

Meat (*carne*) is plentiful. Local Canarian pork (*cerdo*) is excellent: pork chops (*chuleta de cerda*) are on every menu. Beef (*carne de vacca*) is of good quality and imported from Brazil. There is no problem with getting it minced (*carne picada*). Lamb (*cordero*) and mutton (*carne de carnero*) are rather more expensive. Liver (*higado*) and kidneys (*rinon*) are cheap and tasty. Chickens (*pollo*) are plentiful, fresh or frozen. Very succulent is young goat or kid (*cabrito*) which is roasted on special festive occasions. Rabbit (*conejo*) is much used for stews.

Fish (*pescado*) is found in all towns and villages, though sometimes supplies run out early in the day. Prices are high owing to the demand. Varieties include, tuna (*atun*), cod (*bacalad*), hake (*merluza*), swordfish (*espada*), mackerel (*caballa*) and sardines (*sardinas*). It is possible to go to the fishing villages and buy fish straight off the boats but the prices remain high.

Cheese (*queso*) is imported from many countries and Dutch cheese can be bought more cheaply here than in Holland. Goat's cheese (*queso blanco de cabra*) mainly from Hierro, La Palma and Fuerteventura, is particulary flavoursome.

Milk (*leche*) is not often sold fresh, as there are few cows on the islands. Most milk is 'long-life' imported from Holland in cartons or plastic containers. Tinned and powdered milk are also available.

Bread (*pan*) is sold in most supermarkets, but the place to buy really fresh bread, including brown, is a baker's shop (*panadería*). Rolls and bread are light but not crusty as French bread. Cakes may be bought from a *pasteleria*. These do not usually sell bread as well, but have a selection of sweets and chocolates (*confites y bombón*).

Various brands of tea and coffee are on sale, including ground coffee and Nescafé, the latter a little dearer than in the UK. Excellent local and Spanish honey (*meil*) can be bought; the date palm honey (*meil de palma*) has an unusual flavour.

There is plenty of fresh fruit and vegetables. This is best bought in the open markets but supermarkets in the tourist centres are well supplied. The selection is wide, so enjoy fresh strawberries and pineapples at Christmas time!

Local dishes

It is possible to have typical British meals in the Canaries. 'Real English Breakfast' signs are displayed in all tourist resorts. Most hotel restaurants serve food that tends to be bland; trying to please all their customers, they refrain from too much flavour.

Local dishes often include *papas arrugadas* (wrinkled potatoes) — quite delicious little new potatoes cooked in their skins in sea- or salt-water; these should be eaten with their skins on. Served with chops or fish, they will be accompanied by a Canarian piquant sauce called *mojo,* made of oil, vinegar, salt, pimento and spices. *Mojo picon* is red and hot, *mojo verde* is green and milder; often the sauces vary according to the cook. The sauce can be obtained in supermarkets, a small bottle costing about 120 pesetas (60p).

Familiar Spanish dishes include *gazpacho* — a tasty cold soup made from tomatoes, onions, pimentos, olive oil and sherry; and *paella* — rice cooked with saffron to which are added meats, fish and vegetables. *Tortilla* can be a simple omelette; *tortilla española* is when potatoes, onions and vegetables are added.

Canarian soups (*sopa*) are tasty and almost a complete meal, so many good things are included. The one that is recommended to tourists is *sopa de berros,* watercress soup with herbs.

Stews (*puchero* or *estofado*) are considered a main dish; often made with rabbit (*estofado de conjero*), they are eaten with *gofio,* a meal made from wheat or maize which is toasted before being ground, and then made into a sort of dumpling, or sometimes eaten as bread.

Fish stew (*cazuela canaria*) is a fish casserole, with potatoes,

This delightful Canarian fishing family proudly display some of the day's catch at Las Playita, Fuerteventura.

onions, tomatoes, peppers and saffron. Sometimes the fish is cooked whole, the vegetable juices being served first as a soup, then the fish and vegetables are eaten. Try some *pulpo* — better forget that it is octopus, then you will enjoy it!

Chicken (*pollo*) is usually roast (*pollo asado*) on a spit and will be served with chipped potatoes; these are often offered as 'take away' meals.

Desserts (*postre*) are usually fresh fruit (*fruta*), ice cream (*helados*) or *flan,* which is a crème caramel. Mouth watering *gateaux* are filled with strawberries (*fresas*) and cream (*nata*).

Other island specialities are *quesadilias* — cheesecakes from El Hierro, and *rapaduras* — an almond and honey sweet from La Palma.

Our special favourite Canarian foods are:

Cobrito al horno	— roast young goat
Cochinillo asado	— roast suckling pig
Cocido canario	— Canarian stew
Cordornices rellenas	— stuffed quail
Jamón canario	— local ham
Parillada criollo	— charcoal steak

Salmonetes fritos	— fried red mullet
Atun con salsa de tomate	— tunny fish in tomato sauce
Zarzuela	— fish stew
Plátanos a la canaria	— fried banana in brandy sauce
Galletas de almendra	— almond biscuits

Drinks

All the islands produce their own wine but in such small amounts that there is little for the visitor to buy. The best is said to be *vino del monte* from Gran Canaria. Lanzarote's *malvasia* or malmsey wine is in better supply; it can be bought sweet (*dulce*) or dry (*seco*). Tenerife produces a *malvasia* and a *moscatel,* El Hierro has a *vino dulce,* a sweet wine. La Palma's wine is also a *malvasia* and can be purchased sweet or dry. The latter is pleasant when chilled and served as an aperitif.

Plenty of wine is imported from mainland Spain and sells from 195 pesetas (£1) a litre. Good Spanish wines come from Rioja, Valdepenas and Jumilla. Spanish champagne costs from 250 pesetas (£1.28) per bottle.

Wine in Lanzarote

The story of viticulture in Lanzarote is the history of man's struggle against the elements — against a hostile land, strong winds and lack of rainfall. To overcome all these problems, the peasant farmers had to create a system of vine growing that is unique. To shelter the crops from the wind the farmer digs a hole in the ground, sometimes two metres deep, and to combat the lack of water the earth is covered with fine volcanic ash *(picon)* which absorbs and holds moisture from the air. In some areas, semi-circular dry stone walls are built around two or three vines to give extra protection. The island's vineyards total some 3,336 hectares, and they make a strikingly unusual landscape.

Malvasia, which is the famous 'malmsey' referred to by Shakespeare, is grown in the areas of La Geria, Mozaga, Tao and San Bartolomé. The best known labels are El Grifo, Mozaga and Testeyna. All these wine cellars produce dry, semi-dry and sweet malvasia, as well as red and rosé wine, and moscatel. Visits can be made to *bodegas* or wine cellars, for a free taste of the various types of wine. Advice is given to assist your choice, which can then be purchased. Prices range from 450 pesetas (£2.31) per bottle.

The local drink is rum (*ron*) which is distilled throughout the islands and sold in every bar and supermarket. It is a fiery spirit which needs to be tasted with caution. *Ron miel* is a honey rum, similar to a liqueur. As you would expect there is a drink made from bananas: this is a yellow liqueur called *cobana.* Other liqueurs are produced from oranges, pineapples, cherries, almonds and coconuts; assorted bottles of these liqueurs make attractive souvenirs.

As liquor is duty free it is cheap; even whisky is less expensive than in Europe or at duty free shops in airports or ships. It is possible to buy English beer from a keg; however the local beer *(cerveza)* is a light cool drink which is very refreshing at all times. Mineral waters and soft drinks such as Coca-cola and Seven-up are plentiful. The latter drink can be helpful if you have a queasy tummy.

Spanish brandy *(cogñac)* is said to have a less delicate flavour than French brandy. 'Soberano ' and 'Fundador' are two Spanish brandies that are 37° proof, costing about 700 pesetas (£3.60) per litre, and worth tasting. 'Sangria' is a Spanish drink, popular with tourists, that is usually served in a jug for two or more people. It is a mixture of red wine, orange juice, brandy, mineral water, slices of fruit and plenty of ice — refreshingly cool, it can be more potent than it tastes.

Bars and restaurants

In bars it is not necessary to pay for your drinks until you leave, even if you are there all day or night. They never close until the last party leaves. Tipping (called *propina*) is usual. The Spanish eat canapés or appetisers (called *tappas*) when they have a drink; sometimes these are quite elaborate, almost a meal. Lunch is served in restaurants between 1300 and 1500 hrs and dinner from 1930 to 2230 hrs.

It is quite in order for unaccompanied females to use cafés, bars and restaurants. Girl students often sit in a café with a coffee for an hour or so studying their books. Friends will meet at a table in the sunshine for an aperitif, drink a glass of wine, get some olives or peanuts, and no one will hasten their departure. The end of the afternoon is the time when women take a cup of chocolate and *churros* — delicious sweet fritters, freshly cooked. Black coffee is *café solo,* white coffee is *café con leche.*

Tourist offices have lists of recommended restaurants and local newspapers carry plenty of advertisements. Throughout the Canary Islands the choice of type of restaurant or bar is enormous, nowhere could a greater variety of cuisine be enjoyed. Both Lanzarote and Fuerteventura have a few high class hotels with good restaurants, although the choice in Fuerteventura is more limited.

All restaurants in the Canary Islands must display a tourist menu of the day *(menu del dia),* at an average price of 800 pesetas (£4.12); sometimes this includes wine. The menu might be a substantial soup, grilled steak or pork chop, salad, fried potatoes, bread, ice cream or cake. Coffee is always extra. As on the continent, in the Canary Islands food and drink consumed at the bar is cheaper than when ordered from a waiter (*camarero*) and served at a table.

Restaurants are graded into four categories, denoted by the number of forks (*tendores*) shown. The grading reflects the price rather than the quality of the food, with four forks being the highest grade.

The best way to sample local food is to eat where the Canarians gather. Do not be shy of entering, the islanders are well used to seeing tourists about, mostly they take little notice and just get on with their own lives.

Out of town the bars and shops can be unobtrusive, often having half closed doors with maybe a faded Coca-cola sign. Once inside the service will be friendly but not inquisitive.

FIVE

Practical information for visitors

British Consul

Should you be unfortunate and lose your passport it will be useful to know the whereabouts of the nearest British Consul. The British Consulate for Lanzarote is in Arrecife, Calle Rubicon 7. This is a parallel street to Calle José Antonio, where at no. 80 there is a Consular Plaque on the wall giving directions to the Consulate. The office is open Monday to Friday from 1000 to 1200 hrs. Tel: 819528.

Fuerteventura does not have a British Consul. It is suggested that you seek assistance initially from the Tourist Office, Patronato de Turismo, Calle 1st Mayo 33, Puerto del Rosario. Tel: 85 10 24. The office is open Monday to Friday 0830 to 1500 hrs. The Director speaks English.

Budgeting for your holiday

The cost of living should not prove higher in the Canary Islands than Europe or the UK. Generally speaking, package tour holiday-makers require spending money for entertainments, drinks and possibly additional meals, unless the package includes full board. You must allow for extra costs such as taking part in sports and excursions, the hire of chairs and sun umbrellas, laundry, and tips (*propina*) for waiters, taxi drivers and porters (about 10%); and maybe some extra film for the camera and souvenirs.

Prices in tourist areas will probably be a few pesetas higher than elsewhere but if one takes into account the extra cost of travelling to a non-tourist area to do one's shopping, it will probably work out much about the same. For the independent traveller, it is possible to live quite cheaply especially by buying local foods. Chickens, tomatoes, cucumbers, eggs, bread and many drinks are less expensive than in the UK. Bars and restaurants are less costly and give a cheerful and good service.

Chemists

The Spanish for chemist is *farmacia* and they are marked by a green Maltese cross. Unlike in the UK, the chemists in Spain sell only medicants, but they are able to give you medical advice and First Aid. They do not sell toilet requirements. For these you must go to a *drogeria* or *perfumeira.*

In Lanzarote several chemists are to be found in Arrecife, others in Puerto del Carmen, Costa Teguise, Teguise and Yaiza. Generally open from 0900 to 1300 and 1630 to 2000 hrs Monday to Friday, Saturday 0900 to 1200 hrs.

In Fuerteventura there are chemists in Puerto Rosario, Corralejo and Gran Tarajal. As in the UK there will be a chemist open late and on Sundays. The rota should be displayed on the door.

Church services

Most churches in the Canary Islands are Roman Catholic, and in towns and villages it is possible to attend Mass. There are no synagogues in the Canary Islands.

The San Gines Church in Arrecife, Lanzarote holds Mass on weekdays at 1930 hrs and on Sunday at 1030, 1200 and 2000 hrs. An Anglican Chaplain from Las Palmas, Gran Canaria visits Lanzarote every fourth Sunday to hold services in the Catholic and Anglican Church, Nuestra Señora del Carmen, in the old town of Puerto del Carmen. Times of services are 1030 and 2000 hrs but further information should be obtainable from your hotel or apartments reception.

Clothes

You will need lightweight clothes for the Canary Islands. A heavy top coat is not necessary but windcheaters, anoraks and woollen jumpers are essential when visiting high mountain areas. A lightweight raincoat may prove useful.

Generally speaking, loose-fitting cotton and drip-dry garments are the most comfortable. For walking in the hills take stout flat-

Lanzarote's premier Church of San Gines, in Arrecife, has recently been re-consecrated after three years' restoration work.

heeled shoes, as the terrain can be very hard and stony. On the beach rubber flip-flop sandals are useful. Remember that one's feet tend to swell in warm weather so take light footwear.

Sunhats and sunglasses should be used, for the sun in the Canaries is strong and care must be taken to avoid sunstroke.

Evening wear is mostly casual. Some hotels and restaurants require men to wear ties and jackets. When visiting churches it is not essential to wear a hat or scarf but it is expected that you will not be wearing beach clothes. Skimpy clothing is frowned on in towns. Some banks and petrol stations will refuse to serve you if you are not adequately covered.

On beaches bikinis are permitted and topless sunbathing is seen. There are a few places on all the islands where naturists may take their clothes off.

Buying clothes locally

In Lanzarote you will be able to purchase any clothes you may require from a good selection of shops. The main tourist resorts have plenty of boutiques with modern styles. Men's and children's clothes are available, too, in all styles and sizes.

Prices cover a wide range. Many of the Paris fashion houses have shops here and the big stores have whole floors full of all types of clothing including sportswear. Bargain counters with cheaper goods will be marked *rebaja* which means a reduction in price. Sometimes the open air village markets have good bargains but examine the goods to see that they are not shop-soiled.

Being a duty free area it is possible to find oriental silks, furs and leather goods at advantageous prices. When possible it is a good idea to check on the equivalent UK price first.

The range of clothes in the shops of Fuerteventura is more restricted. However it is possible to buy various materials and have clothes made up. In Las Palmas or Tenerife a gentleman's suit can be tailored in 24 hours.

Communications

Post

Post offices (*correos*) similar to those in the UK are in all towns and some villages. Open from 0900 to 1300 hrs. Monday to Saturday, closed on Sunday and Public Holidays.

You may have letters and parcels sent to a local post office for you to collect. They should be addressed to you (surname first, then initials) at Lista de Correos, in the appropriate town (e.g. Lista de Correos, Arrecife, Lanzarote, Canary Islands, Spain). There is no charge for this service. When you collect your mail from the post office you will be required to show your passport.

In shops where you purchase postcards, stamps are usually sold as well. At the time of writing postage to the UK for a letter or postcard costs 45 pesetas (23p). All mail goes by air; parcels can be registered.

The Canary Island post boxes are painted yellow, and are similar in shape to those in the UK. The exception is at main post offices where posting boxes are in the walls of the building. Sometimes they are marked *extranjero* (for posting abroad) and *insular* (for local islands). Small yellow post boxes, square in shape, may be attached to houses in remote country villages.

Telephones

Telephoning from the Canary Islands to the UK or other countries is simple, provided the coin box is not too full to accept further coins. This happens quite frequently in busy tourist centres. Look for a telephone kiosk which says *international;* those marked *urbano* are for local calls only.

You can use 100, 25 or 5 peseta coins, and the directions for use are displayed in several languages near the telephone. In hotels, the switchboard operator will dial your number for you and call you back as soon as the call is through. Some hotels have telephones in the bedroom. A small charge is made for this service.

When using the public telephone, first dial 07 for international calls. Wait for a high pitched continuous sound then dial the code of the country required (for UK this is 44) followed by the subscriber's code and number. In cases where the code starts with 0 it is omitted. For example, if you call London you would dial 44-71 for numbers in the 071 area and 44-81 for numbers with an 081 code. The cost of ringing the UK is around 110 pesetas (57p) per minute.

International country code numbers from the Canary Islands:-

Austria	— 43	Italy	— 39
Denmark	— 45	Portugal	— 351
Germany	— 49	Sweden	— 46
Holland	— 31	UK	— 44

By dialling 9198, it is possible to arrange personal calls. *Cobro revertido* means the recipient of the call pays the cost.

For general information concerning telephones, telegrams, cables and telex, dial 003.

Telegraph

Cable messages can be passed, day or night, by way of the main telephone exchange. Dial 362000.

Telex and fax

For teleprinter service, dial 363717. For emergency remittances, one's own bank at home can send money by teleprinter to a Spanish bank. This service can be granted very quickly. If necessary, ask to use a travel agent's telex. Fax now is generally available.

Dentists

Dentists (*dentista*) are fully qualified, similar to doctors. The service is good and not over expensive. Generally one can call at the surgery, without an appointment, and take one's turn. Hotels and apartments list the nearest dentist. There is a dental clinic at Avenida de las Playas, Las Fariones, Puerto del Carmen, Lanzarote.

Doctors

Doctors (*medicos*) have clinics which are run in a business-like manner. In tourist resorts, there would be an English-speaking receptionist. You usually get immediate attention and pay a fee of about 3000 pesetas (£15) for a visit or consultation. They will give you a receipt for insurance purposes. If you are given a prescription you take it to a chemist (*farmacia*) whose sign is a green Maltese Cross. Unlike in the UK, chemists in Spain sell only medications, not toilet requirements, but they are able to give you advice and first aid.

There are also First Aid Posts *(Casa de Socorro*), which is a national service. These posts are often in the country and the buildings are marked with a red cross and a road sign.

Hotels and apartments will have a list of the nearest doctors. There is a clinic in Lanzarote: Doctor Marín, Avenida de las Playas, Las Fariones, Puerto del Carmen, Lanzarote. Tel: 825911. See also the section on Medical services.

Duty free allowances

The UK customs allowance per adult for duty free goods obtained in the Canary Islands is:

Spirits over 22% volume	1 litre
or, sparkling wines	2 litres
still table wine	2 litres
perfume	66cc/ml
toilet water	250cc/ml
gifts	£32 worth
cigarettes	200
or cigars	50
or tobacco	50g

Electricity, radio and television

Electric current voltage is 220 to 225 AC, occasionally 110 to 125 AC. Plugs are the two round-pin variety.

There are local radio stations in the Canaries. The World Service of the BBC is on short wave. It is possible to hear Radio 4 on long wave, when atmospheric conditions are good.

British television sets are not suitable in the Canary Islands. (Spanish television uses Norma G for black and white and Pall for colour.) Most hotels and many bars have black and white or colour television, and nearly all the programmes are in Spanish and relayed from mainland Spain.

ITN News in English, can be seen on the Canary Island TV, Channel 2 at 1200, Monday to Friday, for ten minutes.

Fire precautions

Fire precautions are observed in the Canary Islands, with public buildings and hotels being inspected for adequate fire escape equipment. Details of emergency exits are shown in each hotel room. Modern fire fighting equipment is located in all places of population.

Hairdressing

Men's barbers are called *barberia* and ladies' salons *peluqueria*. In tourist areas prices are higher than in towns. Most large hotels have their own salons and the standard is generally very good. The Canarians have particularly well groomed hair and frequently use hairdressers.

Health

There are no dangerous animals or poisonous reptiles in the Canaries, not many flies and only a few mosquitos. The spring-like weather is healthy and invigorating. Over indulgence with food and drink can cause discomfort and an upset tummy. It is wise to wash all fruits and salads before eating.

There is no shortage of medications in the Canary Islands, but if you prefer a particular British brand it is wise to take a supply with you. Tap water should not be drunk by visitors unless it is first boiled. Water considered fit for drinking is *agua potable* and unsuitable is *agua non potable*. Bottled water is quite cheap and available at supermarkets: called *agua mineral* it is either aerated (*con gas*) or still (*sin gas*).

Canary tummy is a form of sickness and diarrhoea which may last for a few days. A suitable Spanish medication for this is available from chemists. Should the complaint persist it is advisable to consult a doctor. However cases of upset tummy are not to be expected and most people find the Canary climate will make them feel years younger.

Care should be taken to avoid too much initial exposure to the sun. The wearing of sun hats and sun glasses can be helpful. Remember that the sun's rays are very much stronger here than in the UK, so allow periods of 15 minutes exposure to direct sunlight, at first, to parts of the body not usually exposed. Make sure that plenty of sun lotion is applied. Do not wait until the skin is turning red, that may be too late.

Sunstroke can be very distressing. Symptoms are a severe headache, vomiting and much discomfort. Mild cases require a cool shaded room with plenty of liquid. ('Seven Up' is a helpful drink.) Apply calamine or similar cream to affected parts. If the skin is blistered or the symptoms are not improving, do not hesitate to consult a chemist or doctor. Hotels have the addresses and telephone numbers of the nearest doctor or clinic.

Laundry and dry cleaning

If you wish to have clothes cleaned or laundered *(tintorería y lavenderia),* it is probably easier to use the services of your hotel or apartment. Maids will collect laundry and return it clean the same day, lists of charges are usually put in each room. Dry cleaners are more rare and very busy. Launderettes are only beginning to appear in the major tourist resorts.

With the warm sunshine clothes dry very quickly so drip-dry garments are practical. There are all the usual washing powders and detergents available.

Medical services

Spain is part of the European Community and there are reciprocal arrangements. If you wish to take advantage of these you will need a form EIII, Certificate of Entitlement to Benefits in the EEC, obtainable from your local DHSS Office. You need to produce your Form EIII when you require medical attention.

See also sections on Doctors and Health.

Lanzarote

Hospital Juan de Quesada, Arrecife. Tel: 81 05 00.
Clinica Gonzalez Medina, Garcia Escamez, Arrecife. Tel: 81 13 24.
Red Cross, Coronel Valls de Torre 24, Arrecife. Tel: 81 06 32.

Fuerteventura

Hospital, Carretera General al Aeropuerto. Tel: 85 04 99.
Ambulance, Puerto del Rosario. Tel: 85 03 12.
Red Cross, Avenida Almirante, Carrero Blanco, Puerto del Rosario. Tel: 85 12 76.

Money and banks

The Canary Islands are a part of Spain and therefore the currency is the *peseta*. The coins in use are: 1, 5, 25, 50, 100, 200 and 500 pesetas. Notes are: 1000, 2000, 5000 and 10,000 pesetas.

The 'high street' banks there are the same as in Spain and have names like, Banco de Bilbao, Banco Hispano Americano, Banco de Santander and Banco Central. Opening hours do vary slightly but generally are 0830 to 1400 hrs daily, closing at 1300 on Saturdays;

closed on Sundays and Public Holidays. Most Spanish banks accept Eurocheque cards or equivalent, and international credit cards displaying the sign. Be sure to check with your own bank whether your cheque card is valid for use in Spain (the Canary Islands). When you go to the bank you will need to take your cheque book or traveller's cheques, and your passport. They will probably wish to know where you are staying. One can also cash traveller's cheques and exchange currency in travel agents and hotels. The currency exchange rate is displayed in most banks and travel agents. At the present time it is 194 pesetas to £1, for cheques. A small commission is charged for the transaction. Our experience is that the Banco de Bilbao gives very favourable rates of exchange, accepts Eurocheque and Visa cards and has English-speaking staff.

The larger hotels have deposit boxes or small safes for guests to lock up their valuables. Canarians generally are law abiding but in busy plazas, markets and at fiesta time beware of pickpockets.

Newspapers and books

English daily and Sunday newspapers can be purchased in cities, tourist complexes and at airports, usually a day after publication. Newspapers are about twice the UK price. English books and paperbacks are also available in these places.

The island journal for Lanzarote is called *Lancelot*. It is published bi-monthly, costs 200 pesetas (£1.03) and has separate English and Spanish editions. There is no English newspaper or magazine published in Fuerteventura.

Opticians

Opticians (*optica*) provide a very good service. In towns and tourist centres they are able to test your vision, without charge, and supply the required spectacles in about 48 hours. Generally charges are lower than in the UK, with a very good choice of frames.

Police

There are several types of police in the Canary Islands and Spain. The *Guardia Civil,* who wear a green uniform with a shiny black hat, are armed law enforcement officers. It is advisable not to get involved in a misunderstanding with them, they rarely admit to speaking English and have a great deal of power. The municipal police are the local town and village police, either in brown or dark blue uniforms. The Traffic Police, besides controlling traffic, give assistance with breakdowns and other problems. Their patrol cars are marked *Trafico Policia.* All types of police are approachable and helpful, especially the Traffic Police.

Problems and complaints

Complaints about accommodation should be made on official complaints forms (*hojas de reclamaciones*); tourist establishments should have these or the Tourist Office will provide them.

Usually the receptionist or the public relations representative (*relacions publico*) will be glad to sort out your query, they generally speak English. In extreme cases it may be necessary to go to the municipal police or the Town Hall (*ayuntamiento*). You will find officials pleased to assist, but be patient; the Canarian way of life is not to hurry.

Public conveniences

Public conveniences are few and far between in the Canary Islands. They are marked *aseo* or *servicio,* with *señoras* (ladies) and *caballeros* (gentlemen). Pictographs are also used. Toilets are available at petrol filling stations. It is also possible to use the cloakrooms of a hotel, bar or café although it is better to be a customer as well.

Public conveniences will be found in market (*mercado*) places but they are sometimes austere. Payment for the use of a toilet is not required but it is usual to tip the attendant 25 pesetas.

Taking children to the Canary Islands

Taking young children to the Canary Islands presents no real problems. The Canarians are always interested in children, and indeed look after their own with much love and care.

Hotels, apartments and bungalows have cots and highchairs, sometimes at a small extra charge (for example, 300 pesetas/£1.54 per day for a cot). Play rooms and paddling pools, plus babysitting services, help to make life pleasant for all. There are plenty of toy and clothes shops, baby foods and toilet requirements.

Amusements, train rides, playgrounds, ice creams, beach equipment, all are reasonably priced. Young children are allowed into bars, cafés, restaurants and hotel lounges until late at night. Hotels have courtesy buses to convey you to the nearest beach.

However, care should be taken not to overtire young children, who easily become excited and possibly restless with the change of surroundings. New foods may not appeal but usually staff are understanding and helpful. Do not overdo the amount of fresh fruits or salads at first. Plenty of liquid to drink is sensible.

Young children often go on coach excursions and have a happy time. Do take some toys or games to amuse a toddler, for sitting in a coach will become tedious without some diversion. Use the toilet when the coach makes a stop for this purpose; drivers have to work to a schedule and it is not always possible to make emergency halts on narrow mountain roads.

With plenty of beaches and warm sea water most youngsters are completely happy. Please do not force your child into the sea, use a little encouragement to paddle or sit at the edge, it is not sensible to be 'tough' when a child is nervous of water. Making a sand castle and fetching a bucket of sea water will do a lot towards gaining confidence. Be sure to provide the child with a sun hat and protection for the skin, and do not leave him to play in the sun for too long at a time. Guard carefully against sunburn and sunstroke (see Health section).

Time

Time is the same throughout the Canary Islands. From April to September Summer Time is in force, as in the UK. In winter the Canaries observe GMT, one hour earlier than mainland Spain.

Tipping

A tip (the *propina*) is expected, as in the UK and the Continent, in bars, cafés and restaurants. Even though a service charge may be added, a tip in the region of ten per cent is generally given, perhaps less for a drink at the bar. The Spanish are proud and well-mannered and do not make much of the subject.

Porters, maids and cloak room attendants should also be tipped

25 or 50 pesetas, though porters at airports may have a fixed charge per piece of luggage. Taxi drivers expect a ten per cent tip.

Water

Lanzarote and Fuerteventura have very little in the way of a natural water supply. What there is comes from privately owned wells. In the recent past tankers brought supplies of fresh water from Tenerife. Now there are desalination plants in both islands, which has eased the situation. There are more main water supplies, though some is still delivered by tanker lorries. Desalinated water is safe to drink, but to be on the safe side it is recommended that you buy the bottled water that is sold in all supermarkets and bars. As water on these islands is so precious and costly you are asked not to waste it.

Fishing boats now have a new jetty at Morro Jable, Fuerteventura, and yacht marina facilities are being developed.

SIX

The Canary Islands and the islanders

History of the Canary Islands

The Canary Islands were known to the Ancient World under various names; the Greeks called them 'The Isles of the Blessed' and Homer described them as the location of the 'Elysian Fields'. Later Herodotus writing in the fifth century BC, referred to them as 'The Garden of Hesperides' and the archipelago was generally known to the Romans as 'The Fortunate Islands'. Much of the early history of the Canary Islands is uncertain and is only partly explained in the myths and legends that tell of the first inhabitants' experiences.

It seems likely the Canaries were known to seafarers well before the Spanish colonised the islands in the fifteenth century. The Phoenicians are reputed to have collected 'orchilla', a purple dye, from the islands during their explorations along the coast of North West Africa; they used the dye to colour carpets and clothes. The Roman writer Pliny the Elder (AD 23 to 79) writes of an expedition sent by King Juba the Second of Mauritania to The Fortunate Islands about 30 BC. Pliny tells how Juba's troops found the islands deserted but with many ruins of great buildings. The soldiers saw enormous wild dogs roaming the islands, and they brought two of the animals back to the King. Afterwards the lands became known as the 'Canis Islands', *canis* being the Latin for 'dog', and in later years the 'Islands of Dogs' was corrupted to 'Canaria'. So the collective name of the Canary Islands has nothing to do with the native bird of that name but refers to these wild dogs.

When the Spaniards arrived in the fifteenth century they found a primitive race akin to Stone Age people occupying the islands. How they got there and their origins still remain something of a mystery. The Encyclopaedia Britannica records that the aboriginal inhabitants of the Canary Islands were called Guanches (*Guan* — person, *Chinet* — Tenerife, thus 'Man of Tenerife').

The Guanches

The Guanches, now extinct, appear from their skulls and bones to have resembled the Cro-Magnon race of the Quaternary age. It seems that they may have come from central and southern Europe via North Africa in some distant age. The characteristics of grey-blue eyes and blondish hair still persist in some of the present inhabitants. In the two islands of Tenerife and Gomera the Guanche type has been retained with more purity than in the others. No inscriptions have been found in these islands so it would seem that the Guanches did not know how to write. In all the islands, except these two, Semitic inscriptions and rock signs have been discovered. From these facts it would seem that people from the neighbourhood of Carthage and the Semitic races landed in the Canary Islands.

The Guanches lived in natural caves; they used to paint their bodies and wear garments of goatskin and vegetable fibres, some of which have been found in tombs in Gran Canaria. Necklaces of wood, bone and shells, polished battle axes, lances and clubs are to be seen on display in the various museums in the Canary Islands. Many cave dwellings still exist today in the mountains and remain in daily use, being handed down by each generation and much sought after as part of their heritage.

In Guanche times, many very old people, after bidding farewell to their families, were carried to a sepulchral cave, given a bowl of milk and left to die. Guanches embalmed their bodies and 'mummies' have been found wrapped in goat and sheep skins. In districts where cave dwelling was impossible they built small round houses; their communities were ruled by a king or chief.

They worshipped gods and goddesses, the sun and moon, believed in evil spirits and venerated the rocks and the mountains. Religious festivals took precedence over wars and personal quarrels.

When the Spanish conquered the islands during the fifteenth century, the Guanches are said to have put up heroic resistance against the invaders and many folk tales tell of the bravery of the doomed defenders, who in some instances preferred honourable suicide rather than ignominious defeat.

During the year 999 AD the Arabs landed and traded on Gran Canaria. In the thirteenth and fourteenth centuries Genoese, Majorcan, Portuguese and French navigators visited the islands and had a friendly welcome from the Guanches.

Early in the fourteenth century, Lancellotto Malocello, an Italian nobleman from Genoa, discovered Lanzarote and gave his name to the island when charting a map. Although he exploited the natives for labour he made no attempt to take over the island.

Conquest

The conquest of the Canary Islands by the Spanish lasted nearly a century, starting in 1402. The French nobleman, Jean de Bethancourt, under the commission of the King of Spain, together with another nobleman, Gadifer de Salle, invaded Lanzarote and Fuerteventura. After much struggle they managed to subdue the islands and to a lesser extent also La Gomera and El Hierro.

Ostensibly the Spanish invasion was to spread Christianity but they also took slaves and killed many of the inhabitants who put up a noble resistance. There was much intrigue and fighting amongst the invaders themselves when taking over the islands; this included an interim Portuguese ownership of Lanzarote and Gomera but in 1470 the Portuguese ceded their rights to the Catholic Kings of Spain. Captain Juan Rejon was sent to claim the lands for Spain and stop the fighting. In 1478 Juan Rejon landed in Gran Canaria with Castilian troops; after many cruel battles he was replaced by Pedro de Vera who in April 1483 took over the island for Spain.

Alonso de Lugo and his forces also fought many battles against the Guanches before their resistance was broken. The majority were killed in battle, some taken as slaves, a few were assimilated amongst the invaders. In 1492 La Palma fell, then in 1496 the final battle was fought at La Victoria de Acentejo in Tenerife, so at last the conquest was over and the entire archipelago was incorporated into the Crown of Castile.

Christopher Columbus

When in 1492 Christopher Columbus began his search for the New World, he put into Las Palmas, Gran Canaria for repairs to his ships, and later he sailed on to La Gomera for water and victuals. On future voyages he returned several times to the islands, especially La Gomera, where it is reputed he was enamoured with the beautiful widow Beatriz de Bobadilla, whom he had met previously at the Spanish court.

The Canaries became a useful staging post between Europe and the Americas, but were subject to attacks by pirates from many countries, including the English, Dutch and the Moors who were looking for slaves and timber. During the sixteenth and seventeenth centuries the islands began to prosper with the cultivation of the vine, the production of sugar, and ship repairs. Canary 'sack' or 'malmsey' wine was much sought after by Elizabethan sailors such as Raleigh and Drake. Records show that Thomas Nichols, a 'factor' of an English company which traded in sugar, lived in Tenerife from 1556 to 1571. He wrote a book *The Fortunate Islands,* published in London in 1583.

In 1589 Philip II of Spain created the post of Captain General of the Canaries, fortifications were built as a means of defence and protection from raiding pirates and other invaders. Many of these fortresses remain to this day and form museums of interest to the tourist. So during the following years the islands developed and prospered. But a serious challenge to Spanish sovereignty was made by the British under Lord Nelson in 1797. They were repulsed in the Battle of Santa Cruz de Tenerife, where Nelson lost an arm; one hundred and twenty-three British sailors were wounded and two hundred and twenty-six killed.

The Paisley and Little Company of London carried out a thriving business between 1770 and 1834. They exported Canarian wine and, in return, imported to the Canaries textiles, flour, tobacco and English manufactured goods. Major business houses were established by the late eighteenth century and firms like Yeowards from Liverpool and Elders and Fyffes from London both had banana and shipping trade based on the islands.

Unification with Spain

In 1823 the Canary Islands were united to become a single province of Spain with its capital at Santa Cruz de Tenerife. This caused much annoyance to Gran Canaria, who thought that Las Palmas was of equal importance and deserved the title. The Law of Free Ports was passed in 1852, turning the archipelago into a duty free area and allowing the Canarians to trade with the whole world. Although Spain remained neutral during the First World War, the drop in maritime traffic had a harmful effect on the islands.

In 1927 the archipelago was declared two provinces of Spain, each with its own capital and council. The **Western Province** comprises Tenerife (capital, Santa Cruz de Tenerife), La Gomera, El Hierro and La Palma. The **Eastern Province** comprises Gran Canaria (capital, Las Palmas), Fuerteventura, Lanzarote with the islets of Los Lobos, Graciosa, Montana Clara, Alegranza, Roque del Oeste and Roque del Este. There is still friendly rivalry between the two provinces.

It was while serving as Military Governor of the Canary Islands in 1936 that General Franco plotted then led the anti-Socialist revolt that sparked off the Spanish Civil War, and the Canary Islands were used as a base for training the revolutionary troops.

During the Second World War, Spain and the Canaries remained neutral. After the war, as a result of the development of modern refrigeration and commercial air transport, the agricultural industries of the islands improved. Ports were enlarged to cope with modern shipping, airports were built or enlarged.

The advent of tourism

Tourism which started with a great boom at the beginning of 1970s is now a major industry and an all-the-year-round influx of sun seeking visitors has taken people away from the land to work in hotels and shops. The Canary Islands today with a population of 1,500,000 are peaceful, progressive and working hard for a stable economy.

Canarian way of life

The Canarian way of life is like that in Spain — out-going and friendly. The Canarians like to sing, play music and dance whenever possible. For no reason at all they may greet you and shake hands. To pass a Canarian you know and not greet him is an insult. It is impossible to rush Canarians into taking a decision, but given time they will be pleased to help you, particularly if you are in trouble. Should you ask the way to a place, it is quite likely that you will be taken there, or someone else will be asked to assist you.

They are a proud people who dress well, with hair neatly groomed. They do not like tourists wearing scanty clothing other than on the beaches.

Although the bars and cafés are open all day and do not close until late at night, drunkenness is very rare indeed. Thankfully, there are few cripples or beggars in the streets. Disabled people are employed selling lottery tickets at street corners in the towns. Old people are cared for by their families.

The visitors will notice that the pace of life will seem slower, people do not rush about frantically as in North European countries. The Spanish word *mañana* meaning tomorrow, is often applied — why hurry?

Communal activities are ritualised. The evening gossip, called the *paseo,* is still enjoyed in every town and village, especially in the *plaza mayor* (main square). As the sun begins to set, people walk slowly up and down the streets, the air is filled with cheerful chatter. Children play in the plazas, young girls giggle with friends while at

Mary stops to pick some yellow sonchus, growing wild, that fill the fields near Cotillo (Fuerteventura) in early March.

the corners stand patient lottery ticket sellers and gipsies displaying embroidered tablecloths and souvenirs. The Guardia Civil (police) in their singular black patent-leather hats pace slowly about, always in pairs, their revolvers hanging at the ready. They, too, will stop for a coffee and a chat. Young children are allowed to stay up late so that the whole family can get together in a restaurant or on a park bench. Canarians love their children very much, and are always pleased to talk about them. It is a good form of introduction if you make a pleasant remark about a child.

The islanders consider themselves to be *Canarios,* not Spaniards, whom they refer to as *Peninsulares.* People from Feurteventura are also known as *Majoreros* and those from Lanzarote as *Conejos.*

Although the Spanish culture naturally has a predominating influence, there are also South American, Portuguese and British undertones. The British community has for many years contributed to the business way of life. It is only comparatively recently with the growth of tourism that German and Scandinavian entrepreneurs have infiltrated.

The cheerful Canarians realise that tourism is an economic necessity for them, and their good-natured acceptance of hordes of foreigners is to be admired.

Language

The Canarians speak Spanish. The accent and pronunciation is slightly different in each island but for Spanish speakers there is not much problem with comprehension. Canarians generally make an effort to communicate, and many also speak English, German and French.

Nowadays English is taught as a second language in the higher grade schools. So if you have a query you are more likely to get an answer from a student than from an older person. In the smaller country villages it may be hard to find someone who understands English at all. Thus it is sensible to carry an English/Spanish dictionary and phrase book, also a local map, when seeking directions and information. (See also Appendix A.)

A botanist's paradise

The Canary Islands have been called a botanist's paradise: the physical characteristics of the islands and their climate with little variation between the seasons combine to produce a diversity of environments for a variety of flora, within a relatively small area. The islands are a true Garden of Eden where dark, dense forests give way to heathers, gorses and bracken. Steep green valleys are terraced with eucalyptus, mimosa, cork trees and broom. Lush meadows harbour butterflies, dragonflies and ladybirds amongst the wild marigolds and buttercups. Oases of palm trees give shade for the cultivation of alfalfa, while cineraria and honeysuckle mingle in the hedgerows.

In the populated areas of the islands, in parks and gardens, geraniums, rosy hibiscus, carnations, marigolds, nasturtiums and bougainvillea bring a riot of colour, sometimes growing wild along the verges. The poinsettia, often in double form and of various hues from deep red to pale lemon, grows into thick hedges as high as trees. The exotic strelitzia, the bird of paradise flower with its waxen blue, white and orange blossom, and birdlike shape, has now become established as the Canary Islands' symbolic flower. And one of the greatest delights of the islands is the sweet perfume of the wild aromatic plants and exotic flowers. Laburnums, honeysuckle, broom, eucalyptus, pine, and many more, blend together to create a wonderful nosegay from nature.

About 1,800 different species of plants grow wild. Some have been here since the late Tertiary period: fossilised plants have been discovered, similar to those found in Mediterranean areas dating from that time. One of the last surviving trees of the Tertiary era is the *dracaena draco,* which may be called a living fossil. The tree is known as the dragon tree, or dragon's blood tree, because of the resinous secretions which, when exposed to the air, turn a dark, blood red. The one at Icod de los Vinos in Tenerife is reputed to be at least 3,000 years old. It is a weird sight, with its main thick trunk branching out into many more trunks, and a massive ridged top with spiky green leaves. The Guanches attributed magical powers to the sap of the dragon tree and thought it a cure for various ailments.

Botanical gardens

Each wave of newcomers has introduced new varieties of plants to the Canaries, and since the Middle Ages the islands have been used for acclimatising tropical plant species before taking them to colder climates. The Botanical Gardens in Tenerife and Gran Canaria contain thousands of rare exotic plants and botanical gems from all over the world, as well as endemic species, and these gardens are well worth a visit.

National parks

The **Timanfaya National Park,** in the western part of Lanzarote, is an area of intensive volcanic eruptions dominated by inorganic or mineral components. The lower part of the park is an immense field of solidified lava where vegetal species are only just beginning to colonise the arid ground. Aeonios or semperuivums, and tabaibas, the sturdy euphorbias, can be seen clinging to the bare rocks. These desert plants make welcome patches of green, but Lanzarote's National Park is not the place to go to study flora or fauna! However, on the rest of the island botanists will have plenty to appreciate.

Fuerteventura's **Parque Natural de las Dunas de Corralejo** and the Islas de Lobos are unique for the wind resistant flora which of very recent years, owing to increased rainfall, have developed sturdier plants.

The Teide National park in Tenerife, the Caldera de Taburiente National Park in La Palma and Gomera's Garonjay National Park all have a variety of flora, including many cacti.

Much of the land on Lanzarote is comprised of ash (picon) and cultivation is difficult, but here a cactus-like agave blooms brightly.

Wildlife

The islands' fauna are less numerous than the plants, the most famous being the giant lizards of El Hierro (*lacerta simonyi*) which grow to a length of one metre. Thought to be extinct, they have recently again been discovered, but their whereabouts is a guarded secret. Smaller versions of these lizards, the *tizon,* can sometimes be observed in the drier regions; they are quite harmless. In Lanzarote the Haria lizard is reputed to be of very ancient origin. While on Fuerteventura, in the mountains near Betancuria, an unusual type of squirrel *(ardilla)* is breeding so fast that it has now been declared a pest to be destroyed. There are no poisonous snakes and only a few scorpions, mosquitoes and flies. Rabbits, hares, goats, camels, donkeys and similar animals have been introduced by man.

Bird life is varied. There are over 200 species, some so well adapted to life on the islands that they can fly only short distances. There are many pigeons, partridge, quail, blackbirds, robins and sparrows. Birds of prey such as crows, vultures, buzzards, white eagles and sparrow hawks are seen frequently. Perhaps disappointingly the native Canary bird (*sarinus Canaria*), which is completely yellow when domesticated, is a brownish colour with only touches of yellow in the wild, but its song is still sweet. The Tenerife chaffinch has an iridescent black and blue plumage. But perhaps the most striking bird seen is the hoopoe, whose bold black and white wing pattern, erectile crest, pink-brown plumage and long curved bill, make it instantly recognisable; its 'hoo poo poo' call carries far.

The melody of the bird song can be heard in many parks and gardens all over the islands. The national parks, too, provide ornithologists with much to observe and note.

Migrant birds use the Canary Islands, especially seabirds crossing the Atlantic. Birds from North Africa, too, visit Fuerteventura and the sandy Jandia beaches: little egrets, sandpipers and curlews search the inland saltwater pools for food.

Brilliant butterflies, dragonflies, moths and other small insects breed in the green vegetal areas of the Canaries. The cochineal insect (*coccus cacti*) is bred on the Nopal, a prickly pear type cactus, mainly in Lanzarote; it is used to make the cochineal dye which gives a red colouring to edibles like sweets, toothpaste and lipstick. Transparent-winged cicadas with their shrill chirping, fill the air with the sounds of a tropical night.

One of Lanzarote's most prolific exports, onions, grow well in the black lava soil. This field is bordered by grape vines.

Agriculture

Two important factors influencing climate and, consequently, agriculture in the Canaries are the winds, which blow in from the Atlantic and the north-east (tradewinds), and the Gulf Stream, which flows in to warm the colder Canaries currents. The winds bring clouds which, when they hit the high mountainous areas, condense to give rain. Thus, in those islands which have a central mountainous zone, we find that the northern and western parts are humid and verdant, while the southern parts, beyond the mountains, are drier and less fertile. Much less rain falls on the islands of Lanzarote and Fuerteventura because these are much flatter; besides they are nearer to the coast of Africa and are subject to hot winds blowing from the Sahara.

At one time the economy of the islands rested on the cultivation of sugar cane, but it became unprofitable; then the vine took over — Canary sack and Malvasia were as popular as Madeira — but this too failed. Sugar and wine are still produced but today the main crop is bananas. These are exported all over the world but for economic reasons the main market is Spain. Tomatoes, potatoes and cucumbers are also important exports, and various other vegetables — such as peppers, aubergines and onions — are produced for overseas markets. In recent years the export of flowers, by air, has increased: these are mainly roses, carnations and the islands' brilliant strelitzias. Cereals, salads, greens, beans, apples and pears are cultivated mostly for the local market.

Tobacco is grown, mainly in La Palma, where factories produce cigars which have a high reputation. The cigarette industry is important in both Tenerife and Gran Canaria.

The little Canary banana, *musa cavendishii,* is deliciously sweet, to be enjoyed when there. Sometimes, as with the tomato, it is difficult to purchase the ripe fruit because they are cropped when very green. One frequently encounters huge lorries carrying enormous loads of the heavy 'hands' of green bananas along narrow country roads; they can make travelling very slow.

On all the islands the country people work long and hard, often with hand tools, sometimes assisted by donkeys and camels — an incongruous sight. Modern machinery is gradually being introduced both in the field and packing shed.

A special mention must be made of the great endeavour with which the people of Lanzarote and Fuerteventura cultivate their lands. The persistence of the peasants to produce their crops despite severe water shortages and volcanic soil arouses admiration.

A strange sight are these circles of stones and deep holes, which shelter plants from the strong winds. The volcanic ash is porous and so retains moisture for the vines and fig trees.

Their ingenious method of creating moisture in the land is to dig deep saucers, filling them with volcanic ash, so retaining moisture from the early morning dew to stop the roots from drying out. Sometimes the crops have to be protected from strong winds by windbreaks made from lava stones and grasses. Even so in a dry winter whole fields of crops may wither and die without sufficient moisture. So if you should be on the islands on one of the rare rainy days do not complain too much; rain is so precious and much prayed for by all the Canarians.

Fishing industry

Fish is part of the staple diet of the islanders particularly those who live by the sea. They will often use a boat for inshore fishing during the night. In the early morning the entire family will be on the beach to help pull in the boats and assist with the catch. You can help too!

Many Canarians are involved with sea fishing, the main catches being tuna, swordfish, mackerel and sardine, all of which are used for export and canning. The seas around are full of fish, great shoals are found in the waters that lie between Lanzarote, Fuerteventura and North Africa; but unfortunately some of the fishing fleets are poorly equipped.

Sport fishing is popular in these waters and many world record catches have been made, especially from Puerto Rico, Gran Canaria.

National holidays

Shops and offices are closed on the following national feast or *fiesta* days. Bars, restaurants, theatres and cinemas are open, however, and public transport operates though sometimes the services are limited (as on Sundays).

January	1	— New Year's Day
	6	— Epiphany
March	19	— San José
(variable)		— Good Friday
		— Easter Monday
May	1	— Labour Day
(variable)		— Corpus Christi
(variable)		— Ascension
June	29	— San Pedro and San Pablo
July	18	— National Day
	25	— Santiago Apostal
August	15	— The Assumption
October	12	— Día de la Hispanidad
November	1	— All Saints
December	8	— Immaculate Conception
	25	— Christmas Day

In addition each city, town and village holds religious festivals and *fiestas* for its own patron saints. Christmas (*Navidad*) is celebrated with shops being decorated and there are scenes of the

Nativity and the Three Wise Kings, for it is mainly a religious festival.

December 31st (*Noche Vieja*) is much enjoyed with parties, bonfires and fireworks. At midnight the New Year is heralded with the eating of twelve grapes, one at each strike of the clock, amidst great merriment and hooting of car horns and ships' sirens.

January 6th is the day for religious services, then the giving of presents — the most exciting day of the year for all children. Families dress in their best clothes and parade the streets and plazas, with the children showing off their new toys.

Fiestas and festivals

These are taken very seriously in the Canary Islands; religious services and processions are full of fervour. Visitors are always allowed to join in the procession and are made welcome if due respect is observed.

Calendar of fiestas

Fuerteventura

February	2	Celebrations to honour the Virgin of Candelaria (La Oliva)
February		Carnival
May	2	Fiesta Maria Auxiliadora, Montaña Blanca.
July	14	Fiesta del patron San Buenaventura (Betancuria).
July	16	Fiesta de la Virgen del Carmen (Corralejo)
September	8	Our Lady of La Antigua
September		(Third Saturday) Fiesta de la Virgen de la Pena, (Betancuria)
October	1-6	Fiesta de la Virgen Rosario (Puerto del Rosario)
	10-13	Fiesta de San Miguel (Gran Tarajal)

Lanzarote

January	4	Cabalgata de los Reyes Magos (Teguise)
February		Carnival (Arrecife)
June		(variable) Corpus Christi procession (Arrecife)
June	24	Fiesta da San Juan (Haria)
	29	Fiesta de San Pedro (Maguez)
July	7	Fiesta de San Marcial del Rubicón (Playa Blanco Sur)

July	16	Fiesta de la Nuestra Señora del Carmen (Teguise)
August		All the month Fiesta de San Gines (all island). Traditional dancing, camel drawn carts.
August	24	Fiesta de San Bartolomé
September	8	Fiesta de Nuestra Señora Guadalupe (Teguise)
	15	Fiesta de la Virgen de los Volcanes (Tinajo)
November	30	Fiesta San Andres, Tao
December	4	Fiesta Santa Barbara, Máguez

Folklore

Canary folklore thrives with the different islands keeping to their own traditions. This is very noticeable in the varying styles of dress, singing and dancing. Religious fiestas often begin with the *Romeria* (pilgrimage), a long procession of people with gaily decorated horses and carts; in Lanzarote camel drawn carts are used.

Special programmes for each town are preserved and presented each year. Acrobats, clowns and dwarfs perform in the street, great battles are re-enacted with much vigour. In Santa Cruz de la Palma, the Fiesta of the Descent of the Virgin has taken place uninterruptedly for three hundred years.

Amongst the Lanzarote festivities are several highlights. One is the Arrecife Corpus Christi processions in June, when the plaza and streets around the Church of San Gines are decorated with religious paintings and colourful patterns created on the ground using dyed salt. Another is in February at Carnival time, when two traditional groups of dancers, Los Diables de Teguise and Los Buches, dance through the streets beating the inflated stomachs of fish.

Canary music and dancing

The Canarians are a musical people, who love to sing and dance on every occasion. From a very early age toddlers are encouraged to make music; visitors to the islands are charmed to see tiny children who clap their hands and sing to a natural rhythm while at play.

Each island has its own folk dances and songs, but the general influence is Spanish and South American. The flute and tambourine are popular but the islands' most typical instrument is the *timple.* Much like a small guitar or ukelele, the *timple* was first made at Teguise in Lanzarote where there are still craftsmen making this delightful instrument.

Canary folk song and dances have a typical swaying movement, with languid drawn out melodies; gestures and brightly coloured costumes combine to make a unique and exotic impression. The *folia* is slow, the man demonstrating his feelings for the woman with dignity and restraint. *Folia* songs have been compared with the Portuguese *fado*. The *isa* is a light and gay dance similar to an English country dance.

The costumes worn by men and women are highly decorative. The women wear bright coloured, often striped, skirts over long white petticoats; sometimes the overskirts are delicately embroidered and looped up. Dainty lace-trimmed aprons and embroidered waistcoats fit neatly over white blouses with large puff sleeves. Black ankle boots, scarves and hat complete the picture. It is the type of hat which helps to identify the islander: in the eastern islands, the scarf covers the face more and the hat is wider brimmed. In Tenerife and La Palma the hat is tilted towards the back of the head.

The men's costumes include white shirts, black knee length trousers over white underbreeches, long red waistcoats and colourful cummerbunds or sashes. Woollen knee-length socks and white spats over black shoes are worn and a soft black felt hat. Sometimes a thick cape completes the costume.

Students from various Spanish universities can frequently be seen in carnival costume, singing and playing in bars, restaurants and plazas to collect money for charity.

At fiesta time glittering masks are sold, and everyone delights in dressing up. Young girls paint their faces and nails, flashing smiles in all directions, and young men wear flowing capes and carry guitars.

Exhibitions and galas of Canarian music and folk dancing are held regularly on all the islands, throughout the year. Some are planned for the tourist, but most are for the delight of the happy Canarians, whose greatest pleasure is to make music and dance.

Handicrafts

All the islands retain many craftsmen and women, in some instances their skills are unique. Craftsmanship has played an important part in architecture as can be seen in the old Canary houses and churches. Implements like yokes and ploughs, kitchen utensils, beautiful looms for weaving, furniture, cedar chests and pipes for smoking, all have over the years been carefully carved from the many different types of wood growing locally. Musical instruments,

Canarians love fiesta times and celebrate with music and dancing in the streets. Men and women wear highly decorative costumes which vary from island to island.

too, like the Canarian guitar (*timple*) and castanets (*chacaras*) are still being made by traditional methods.

The typical Canary **basketwork** has its origin in its use for agriculture. *Vara* (twig) basketwork is very sturdy; made from strips of young wood like chestnut, in La Palma it reaches an outstanding quality, whilst in Tenerife it is executed with darker, wider and thicker strips of wood.

Cana (cane) basketwork can be pure cane for making delicate baskets, or a mixture of cane and twig for strength. *Palanqueta,* where strips are obtained from the stalks of bunches of dates, gives a highly decorative effect. Very sturdy baskets are made on the island of Hierro, especially at Sabinosa.

Other basketwork produces hats, mats and handbags made from the palm leaf. The central stem of the palm, the *purgano,* can be used for fans and brooms. In Ingenio, Gran Canaria another strong basket is made from reeds. Straw can be used on its own or tied with bramble, to make hampers and containers for dried fruit. Each island keeps to its own traditional work.

There is renewed interest amongst the young in the ancient arts, especially amongst potters who work alongside the old crafts people. The main characteristics of typical Canary **pottery** is its simplicity and non use of the wheel, the craftsman's hands being the only means of lifting and rotating the clay. A small amount of sand is put under the clay to stop it adhering to the ground or bench.

It is fascinating to watch the work of someone like Dona Guadalupe Nubla, in the village of Chipude tucked away in the craggy mountains of Gomera. The shapes of the pots remain the same as in Guanche times.

The pottery being produced in Lanzarote is yet another form of art, as created by Juan Brito, whose style is more abstract. Also on Lanzarote is a famous potter, Dona Dorotea, a wonderful old lady of ninety years who lives in the north of the island near Muñique. She has been making pottery since she was a girl and was taught by her mother, who was, in turn, taught by her mother, using a primitive form of art. The clay is brought from the nearby cliffs at Farmara. She works in a simple stone shed and forms the figures with her hands, without any form of potter's wheel. The work is then dried in the sun and later baked on a metal frame over a fire of twigs and small corncobs. Each piece of her work is signed and no two pieces are identical. In La Palma, the Benahorita people (the ancient inhabitants) bequeathed a unique type of pottery which has a wonderful glaze, and is marked with prehistoric spirals and geometrical designs.

Weaving is still worked on handlooms. Traditional *traperas* rugs, made from rags, are sometimes now woven with wool. Always in bright colours, they make lovely souvenir presents. Among the places where you can see this work done is the *artesania* (craftshop) near Hermigua in Gomera. At El Paso in La Palma you can find a unique example of silk weaving.

Wonderful silk shawls decorated with delicate **hand embroidery** can also be found in La Palma. The *bordados* tablecloths of La Palma are of such a high standard of craft that they are considered amongst the finest work of the islands. Although expensive to purchase they make magnificent heirlooms.

The handicraft that tourists can most easily observe and purchase is **open threadwork** (*calados*). The work is done mainly in Tenerife, Gran Canaria and Fuerteventura, but it is a cottage industry pursued when conditions do not allow work in the fields. *Calcados* is executed by stretching the cloth on a frame, and drawing the threads together to form an intricate pattern. Usually each piece is worked by more than one person. Each island has its own designs and it is interesting to compare these. The same patterns appear on the blouses and skirts worn by the folk dancers.

Various schools of needlework throughout the islands are now open to visitors and the articles sold there are usually a little less expensive than in the shops. Seeing pretty young twelve-year-olds patiently working their needle must surely make you reach for your purse to keep alive the art of hand embroidery.

It is impossible to write about the preservation of handicrafts and traditions in the Canaries, without mentioning the work of Cesar Manrique. Born in Lanzarote he is an artist and sculptor of international renown. Lanzarote has become an ecological focus point for the way he has protected the environment and harmonised new developments with the landscape. He consistently opposes high rise apartments, bill posters, advertisement boardings and rubbish in Lanzarote. It was he who designed the superb Lago Martinez of which the people of Tenerife are justly proud.

The list of handicrafts of the islands is long, and one must mention a few more: delicate lace work done by the convent sisters, rag dolls dressed in typical costume, woollen shawls, native clay figures, polished volcanic stones. (The *peridot* is a green semi precious stone which is made into attractive jewellery.)

Thanks to the patience of the islanders and the support of many tourists, the folklore and crafts are being preserved.

SEVEN

Introducing Lanzarote

Lanzarote is the lowest lying of the seven major Canary Islands, with a maximum height of 671 m at **Penas del Chache** in the Famara range of mountains. It is the fourth largest island, with an area of approximately 806 sq km and a population of 50,000. It is the most easterly of the Canary Islands, the closest to Africa, and also the most northerly of the main islands. Five smaller islands, Graciosa, Del Este, Alegranza, Montana Clara and Roques del Oeste belong to Lanzarote.

Fire Island

Lanzarote is known as the Isla del Fuego (Fire Island). Three quarters of the island is covered with volcanic lava thrown up by a multitude of volcanoes during different periods. The volcanic zone of a past eruption, which took place between 1730 and 1736, has now been designated the National Park of Timanfaya in the Montañas del Fuego (the Fire Mountains), so called because of the emanations of heat which are still present.

Because of its relative flatness, it seldom rains in Lanzarote and clouds are rare, except at times when the *sirocco* wind blows dust from the Sahara. Like most of the islands it has a range of mountains — here they run northeast to southwest — but because they are of no great height they do not attract much moisture. The coasts are mainly level, many have fine sandy beaches or rocky pools.

Lanzarote is said to be named after a Genoese sailor called Lancellotto Malocello who gained a foothold in the fourteenth century. Early Latin maps referred to the island as Insula de Lanzaotus, the Latin equivalent of the mariner's name.

The main impression of the island is of the contrasts between its natural and man-made beauty. The natural volcanic wonders are immensely impressive and vary considerably in different parts of the island, in places creating a lunar landscape quite incredible until seen. But equally notable is the way the inhabitants of this unusual country have clung to their land. With the passage of time, man seems to be able to adapt to the most unlikely of environments and the praiseworthy endeavours of the islanders of Lanzarote are as great an attraction as the wonders of nature.

The capital is Arrecife, a busy port with a fish-canning industry and a huge desalination plant which is the life blood of the island, turning the sea water into the much needed drinking water for daily use. Arrecife is a sprawling town, and at this point of time rather a mess of re-building, but one is hopeful that given a few more years it will be as attractive as the rest of Lanzarote.

During the last twelve years tourism has progressed successfully: ocean-going cruise ships are able to dock, car and passenger ferries arrive regularly. A modern airport provides a frequent service to the UK and the rest of Europe. Most of the tourist complexes are in the south, where the best beaches are found, but other holiday areas are dotted towards the northern end of the island. Luxury hotels and apartments, restaurants and entertainments of international quality maintain a high standard.

Much credit for all this can be attributed to one man, César Manrique, born in Lanzarote in 1920, an artist and sculptor who has studied and worked all over the world. The love he has for his native land has inspired him to integrate tourism with, rather than impose it upon, the vast wilderness of Lanzarote. As artistic consultant to the Cabildo (local government) he has produced outstanding modern designs which seem to achieve perfect harmony with the natural surroundings and indeed, in places even enhance them. The fact that the islanders themselves appreciate his ideas and speak so highly of him, is significant. Lanzarote is amazingly clean and tidy, even the smallest villages have a neat appearance. Thanks to César Manrique, no large advertisements are displayed, no

(Opposite) *Viewed from the Mirador del Rio on Lanzarote, the small island of Graciosa stands out clearly. Isla de Monte Clara is in the background.* **(Overleaf)** *Black lava soil, white houses with green woodwork and many colourful plants make Yaiza* **(above)** *one of the prettiest villages. Palm trees give it a flavour of North Africa. This old drawbridge* **(below)** *leads from the modern buildings of Arrecife to the Castillo de San Gabriel: a link with the time of pirate invasions.*

buildings, except in the capital Arrecife, can be more than four storeys high. Litter is not allowed on the beaches or in the streets. The local population takes immense pride in the 'ideal' situation which is being created.

Despite the lack of rainfall and poor agricultural soil, the people of Lanzarote contrive to produce onions, tomatoes and potatoes for export. Also grown are melons, peas, beans, lentils, chickpeas and maize. The wine of the island (*Malvasia*) is good, rather like dry sherry, and can be 17° proof. Sufficient is produced for it to be exported.

Practically none of the cultivation is irrigated, so it must rely on what rainfall and moisture there is. The people have overcome this difficulty by covering the soil with black volcanic ash to a depth of about ten to fifteen centimetres. The ash stops evaporation and also absorbs the early morning dew, which provides moisture for the underlying soil. The soil and ash have to be replaced every twenty to thirty years. All round the island the pattern of the landscape is black ash, small volcanic humps and oases of neat white modern buildings, with green palm trees making a graceful contrast to the sharper outlines.

Fishing helps the Lanzarote economy. The fleet operates mainly off the neighbouring coast of North Africa. Large salt pans at Janubio produce about 10,000 tons annually and most of it is used in the conservation of fish, though it is also refined and used for kitchen and table salt.

Tenerife and Gran Canaria were, until recently, the only islands with full holiday facilities. Now Lanzarote is in third place and fast developing. It aims to attract a discerning public and holidaymakers will find a harmonious island, full of comfort and spectacular attractions. The island provides varied opportunities for water sports: deep sea fishing, yacht sailing and wind surfing; scuba diving in the clear waters, which contain a variety of underwater marine life. It is on record that no dangerous fish, such as shark, have been seen close to the shores.

History of Lanzarote

Lanzarote and the adjacent isles, including Fuerteventura, were long ago known as the *Purpurarias,* after the Orchilla, which was collected to make a purple dye. The original inhabitants were the Guanches, thought to be of North African origin. The first real European foothold here was secured by the Genoese in the fourteenth century but it was finally taken over by the French invader, Jean de Bethencourt, in the fifteenth century, under orders from Spain. Since then Lanzarote has belonged to Spain.

However the island was subsequently the victim of many pirate raids. The Portuguese, Diego de Silva, attacked the island in 1459 but he tempered his aggression and married a daughter of the Lord of Lanzarote, Diego Garćia de Herrea. The famous Frenchman known as 'Peg Leg' ransacked Arrecife and Arals Calafat landed in 1569 and took some two hundred slaves. In 1617, even the British under Sir Walter Raleigh carried out a raid. A year later the Algerians, Tabac and Soliman, with over thirty ships, landed and took almost a thousand prisoners. The people of Lanzarote had constantly to take refuge in fortresses or to hide in caves.

With the eruption of the volcano, Timanfaya, in 1730 came an even worse disaster, for eruptions continued for six years, destroying over a quarter of the island with lava and ash. Only the stoic tenacity of the inhabitants enabled them to survive. Despite the *malpais* (literally 'bad lands') of volcanic waste, the inhabitants toiled at fishing and agriculture, using donkeys and camels plus human endeavour, to create a way of life.

Today, with half the population living in Arrecife, tourism is being developed into a major industry. With its wonderful climate and the friendly nature of its inhabitants, its large range of facilities, beaches, sport and leisure centres, and some amazing natural wonders, Lanzarote must surely be one of the most 'original' of holiday destinations.

Climate

Lanzarote is similar to the other Canary Islands, with spring like weather all year round. The absence of any large central mountain means that the difference in temperature between the north and the south is minimal. In summer the maximum temperature is 25°C and in winter the average is 17°C.

Although winters are mild the warm clouds sometimes collect on the mountains of the north and fog can form over the Riscos de Famara. In recent years the apparent change in pattern of world wide weather has brought a slightly higher than average rainfall. This of course has been beneficial to this normally arid climate. It has also created a greener landscape in certain parts of the island.

Spring and summer can be windy in Lanzarote, reaching 23 knots or more, which makes it very popular for windsurfers. An easterly wind known as *sirocco* sometimes blows from the Sahara Desert. The temperature rises and it can become oppressive. However these conditions never last long and soon it is back to clear skies again. Should you be experiencing cloudy weather in your resort it is quite likely that in another part of the island it will be sunny. Winter in Lanzarote is generally ten per cent warmer than on mainland Spain.

What to wear

Lightweight clothes are worn all year round. A windproof jacket or cardigan for windy days or a rare cool evening may be required. Bikinis are worn only on the beach. In hotels it is useful to have a robe to wear over swim clothes, when going for a dip in the pool. Casual or trendy clothes are worn in the evening. It is not necessary to wear full evening dress.

The growing popularity of nudism has led to the establishment of a centre for enthusiasts at Charco de Palo Club at **Castillo de Papagayo** in Mala (Haria). Another is under construction at Guatiza.

Places of special interest

Some of Lanzarote's places of special interest are briefly described here. They are described more fully in the island tours (Chapter 10). Approximate distances are given from Arrecife, the capital.

Arrecife (Capital) Main port and busy, friendly town. Ancient fort. Hotels, apartments, shops, small market, restaurants, bars. Promenade, small sandy beach on edge of harbour, yacht club, sailing.

Costa Teguise (9km) East coast, designated for major residential and tourist development. Modern bungalows and apartments. Five-star Melia Salinas hotel. Golf, tennis, swimming, sports clubs. Supermarket, small sandy beach at Los Charcos.

Cuevas de los Verdes (28km) In north, six kilometres of volcanic caves. many open to the public, conducted tour of passages once used by the Guanches.

El Golfo (32km) On south west coast, wide bay formed by volcanic crater, impressive strata, lagoon bright green from microscopic organisms. Pebble beach, rocks. Parking, no bars.

Haria (30km) Pleasant small town in north amid oasis of palm trees. Restaurants, bars. Agriculture, wild flowers. Mirador (4km south) gives extensive views.

Jameos del Agua (30km) Underground cavern 225m long, recently built theatre. Lagoon formed by infiltration of the sea, in which are unique tiny white crabs. Marvellous decor, cactus, ferns and exotic plants. Bar restaurant, small swimming pool. Nightclub.

La Caleta de Famara (25km) Remote pebble, sand and shell beaches on north-west coast, small tourist development. Quiet fishing village, goats, simple small bar-restaurants.

La Graciosa (Orzola 37km) Islet off north coast, day trips from Orzola. Sandy beaches, water sports, fishing. Land Rover tour of islet.

Los Hervideros (29km) Spectacular craggy volcanic caverns, where raging seas send up huge white spumes.

Los Pocillos (11km) Large sandy beach at edge of tourist area. Accommodation. Clear water for swimming.

Mirador del Rio (37km) Extreme north, high look out point and attractive modern restaurant. Good views of small islets. Car park.

Mozaga (11km) In centre of island at crossroads. Modern monument to honour peasants of Lanzarote, by Cesar Manrique, Museum and restaurant. Bodega for wine tasting.

Papagayo (40km) At southern tip, splendid beach but difficult access over sand dunes and dirt road. Worth the effort in suitable vehicle. No facilities on beach. Very tranquil setting.

Playa Blanca (40km) With a good sunshine record, this once tiny fishing village and port is now being developed into a major tourist region. Fish restaurants, supermarkets and ferries to Fuerteventura.

Puerto del Carmen (15km) Centre of tourist activities, south-east coast. Hotels, apartments, villas, shopping. Sports, entertainments. Happy family location.

Salinas de Janubio Large saltpans on south-west coast salt water lagoon, visited by migratory sea birds.

Teguise (12km) Old capital of island, in north central. Ancient church and historic buildings. Narrow streets. Nearby volcanic summit Guanapay. Sixteenth-century fort, Santa Barbara.

Timanfaya National Park (34km) Most spectacular sight on island. Area of approximately 200 sq kms covered with lava rock and ashes from eruption. Fire mountain trip includes demonstrations of steam and heat from ground, coach tour in strange lunar-like landscape.

Salt flats at Janubio, in various stages of drying. In the spring Corpus Christi festival salt which has been dyed various colours is used to create wonderful religious pictures in the streets of Arrecife.

Camel ride up side of volcano. Restaurant. Very awesome and impressive.

Yaiza (23km) In south of island. Delightful tidy little North African-style town, encased in black lava ashes. Church, tourist shops and restaurants. Colourful and interesting.

Zonzamas Ruins (8km) Ancient Guanche fortress, mostly underground and locked. Between Tahice and San Bartolomé.

Beaches

Lanzarote has beaches around most of the coast line, but not all are accessible by road. These *playas* vary from yellow sands to black volcanic sand and of recent years some manmade seashores of imported golden sand have been created. Here we give a short description of the more accessible beaches.

Costa Teguise Playas Bastian, Charcos, Cucharias, El Jabillo and Roca are all manmade yellow sand beaches, very easily reached, in front of the hotels and apartments, and usually are safe for swimming.

From the high cliffs above Playa Famara the view extends to the sandy beach of La Caleta.

Playa Blanca Playas Blanca, Mujeres, Los Pozos, Papagayo and Muelas are all golden sand. The latter is an unofficial nudist beach. Here you have to be careful of the strong currents. Las Colorada and De Afe are more stony. West of Playa Blanca is Playa Flamingo, with manmade, safe, yellow sands, a good place for children. Playa Montaña Roja and a series of sandy coves out towards Punta Pechiguera are being developed.

Puerto del Carmen Playas Guasimeta, Mata Gorda, Los Pocillos, Honda and Puerto del Carmen, are all beaches south of the airport, with Los Pocillos and Puerto del Carmen being the best for safe and pleasant family swimming.

Other beaches around the island

Playa Quemada is on the south coast between Puerto del Carmen and Playa Blanca. At first there's a rocky beach, then at **Playa de la Arena** it flattens to darkish sands that are little visited.

Playa de Famara and **La Caleta de Famara** are in the north west of Lanzarote, with the spectacular Risco de Famara cliffs in the background. Famara is a golden beach six kilometres long and La Caleta has yellow sand and rocks. The sea can be very rough here if it is windy, so it is popular with expert windsurfers. A good beach to 'get away from it all', with fish restaurants nearby.

El Golfo is a small stony, black sand beach on the west coast. It is visited because of its inland green, unfathomable pool of water and the dramatic strata of the volcanic cliffs.

Playa Garita on the east coast by an undeveloped village, has black pebbles and a little golden sandy beach.

Caleta del Mojon Blanco, Caleton Blanco and **Charca de la Lala** are located on the extreme north east coast amongst volcanic rocks. These small patches of sand make good picnic places if the weather is not too hot. Clear pools of sea water are fun for the children. Here you are likely to see the locals fishing for octopus. Good scrambling beaches, but beware of tar.

La Graciosa is a little island which has super beaches and sand dunes; but first you have to get there by boat from Orzola. There are no roads about the island. Playa de Conchas is a golden sand beach amongst volcanic boulders, but is a long walk, taking about two hours to reach.

Playas Reducto and **Del Cable** (Arrecife) are beaches of natural, yellowish sand. At present they are little used, except at weekends by the locals for fishing off the rocks. The sea water by the capital is low lying and, when the tide is out, the beaches appear to be subject to some pollution.

Accommodation

Lanzarote does not have a Parador Nacional. A choice of hotels and apartments, ranging from luxury to simple pensions, can be found in Puerto del Carmen, Costa Teguise and Playa Blanca, with a limited selection in Arrecife. A list of accommodation can be obtained from the Spanish National Tourist Office, 57/58 St James's Street, London W1. Tel: 071-499 0901. But because of the fast opening rate of new hotels, the list is not always complete.

Arrecife

★★★★Hotel — Arrecife Gran Avenida Mancomunidad. Tel: 81 12 50. 286 beds, lift, TV, reading room, night club, tennis, swimming pool, sauna, air-conditioning and garden. On seafront. This is a good Spanish hotel for those who like to be on the edge of a town.

★★★Hotel — Miramar Coll 2. Tel: 81 04 38. 170 beds, breakfast only, bar and lifts. In the centre of town along the seafront, clean hotel with few facilities.

★★★Apartments — Arrecife Playa Avenida Mancomunidad 4. Tel: 81 03 00. 60 apartments, supermarket, restaurant and bar. Good position on edge of town.

★★Apartments — Avenida Avenida Mancomunidad 30. Tel: 81 16 00. 24 apartments but no facilities.

★★Pension — Cardona Calle 18 de Julio 11. Tel: 81 10 08. 111 beds, breakfast only. Near seafront behind Arrecife Gran Hotel.

★Pension — Alespa Calle León y Castillo 50. Tel: 81 18 56. 25 beds, no restaurant, in main city shopping street.

Costa Teguise

★★★★★Hotel — Melia Las Salinas Costa Teguise. Tel: 81 30 40. 591 beds and suites, seaview. A de luxe hotel of the highest grade with a friendly service. It is the epitome of luxury and comfort. Outside are tall palm trees, tropical gardens and a large swimming pool that looks like a lake. The balconies drip with scarlet geraniums and bougainvillea that blend with the white cantilevered building. Inside the marble hall leads to a water garden open to the sky, with trickling waterfalls. Huge green plants trail from containers above from three floors. At night subtle coloured lighting enhances the cool effect. Included in the price of your room are many facilities. Evening brings piano entertainment, cabaret, folk dancing, flamenco dancing and disco club. The restaurant and grill room are first class.

★★★★**Apartments — Lanzarote Gardens** Costa Teguise. Tel: 81 61 00. A newly built and attractive complex of 221 apartments and 21 bungalows which contain bedroom, living room, kitchen, fridge, bathroom, safe and terrace. The large restaurant has a snack bar on the outside terrace by the pleasant, heated swimming pool. There is tennis and squash court. A friendly manager and staff speak English and are very helpful. Private parking and a supermarket close by.

★★★★**Apartments — Los Zocos Club Resort** Costa Teguise. Tel: 81 58 17. 200 one-bedroom apartments with sun terrace, facing four swimming pools and gardens. A modern, youthful complex. The main building has a glass domed roof with interesting light and sound effects. Starcruiser Club for children. There is plenty of entertainment, video club, coffee shop, buffet style and upmarket restaurant. A chemist, gift shop and doctor's surgery are in the same complex.

Puerto del Carmen

★★★★**Hotel — Fariones Playa** Roque del Oeste. Tel: 51 01 75. 449 beds with seaview, airconditioning and music in rooms, lifts, nightclub, swimming pool, sauna, gymnasium, tennis, TV and reading room, conference room, nursery and gardens. A well established and gracious hotel at the western end of the promenade, it has a quiet atmosphere and is used by many Scandinavians.

★★★★**Hotel — San Antonio** Playa de los Pocillos. Tel: 82 50 50. 627 beds, seaview, lifts, suites, airconditioning, TV and music in rooms, swimming pools and sunterrace. Private beach, tropical gardens, tennis courts with instructor, minigolf, nursery, resident doctor, facilities for the disabled, disco, nightclub, shops and hairdressing. A Hocasa hotel with a strong British clientele, it is well appointed and friendly. There is a carpark.

★★★**Apartments — Barcarola** Avenida Maritima de las Playas. Tel: 82 58 00. 141 apartments. Reception, swimming pool, garden and supermarket. It is close to beach and shops.

★★★**Apartments — Coral Club** Calle Grecia. 50 apartments, reception, bar, swimming pool and pleasant gardens. Parking and nearby supermarket.

★★★**Apartments — Olivina Club** Urbanización Costa Luz. 123

apartments, reception, bar, restaurant, music and swimming pool. Close to San Antonio Hotel and beach.
★★**Pension — Magec** Calle Hierro 8. Tel: 22 58 74. 17 beds, no restaurant facilities.

Playa Blanca

★★★★**Hotel — Lanzarote Princess** Playa Blanca. Tel: 83 00 00. 32 mini suites and 407 rooms. A recently built and modern hotel with a spacious, comfortable and relaxing atmosphere. Heated swimming pools, large sunbathing area, tennis, squash courts, minigolf and children's playground. Buffet restaurant, tropical bar and barbecue lunches outside. TV room, dancing, Flamenco Bar open until 0500 hrs, hairdresser, daily animation programme and Happy Hour from 1700 to 1800 hr. A ten-minute, downhill walk to the centre of Playa Blanca.
★★★★**Hotel — Playa Dorada** Playa Blanca. Tel: 20 21 22. 350 beds, all rooms with seaview and generous balcony. A newly opened and well designed hotel by the beach, with a splendid view to the north of Fuerteventura and the island of Los Lobos. A fifteen-minute walk into the centre of Playa Blanca.
★★★**Apartments — Bahia Blanca Rock** Playa Blanca. Tel: 81 61 00. 200 apartments with good size balcony and double bedroom. Swimming pool or seaview, special breakfast in Moby Dick bar but no restaurant. This is a cheerful, youthful complex with a highly praised, attentive manager and staff. Tropical gardens surround a heated swimming pool. Private car parking and supermarket adjacent.

Getting about

Roads

Lanzarote's tarmac roads are good and to travel on them is no problem. They are still improving their road systems, particularly at the junctions. A ring road *(circunvalacion)* round Arrecife is signposted. If you are travelling from Costa Teguise to Puerto del Carmen or Yaiza (or vice versa), it is advisable to use the ring road to avoid the traffic congestion of the city, where cars are to be found parked everywhere. (Usually there is space on the official carpark over the bridge at Castillo San Gabriel where an attendant expects payment of 50 pesetas.)

Many minor roads are narrow and roughly surfaced. One needs to use them to tour the island, so do not expect to travel fast. You

New roads with well-marked junctions are making driving easier on the island. In the distance are the white houses of Uga.

will find sufficient petrol filling stations on the island, but some are closed on Sunday (and public holidays) so top up your tank on Saturday.

Buses

The bus station for Transportes Lanzarote is in the Calle Garcia Escámez 71, Arrecife. Tel: 81 15 46. This is to the north west of the town and is on the main road to San Bartolomé from Arrecife.

Buses run to all the main places and the services are being increased. At present the service between Arrecife and the Costa Teguise is almost hourly, between Arrecife and Puerto del Carmen half hourly, but to Playa Blanca (Yaiza) there are only three buses a day. There are generally fewer services on Saturday, Sunday and public holidays *(festivos)*.

A special service on Sunday to the Teguise market leaves Arrecife at 10.30hrs, returning from Teguise at 1300hrs. Bus fares are not expensive, for example the single fare from Arrecife to Puerto del Carmen is 100 pesetas (£0.51); to Playa Blanca 150 pesetas (£0.77).

The bus stop in Arrecife for Puerto del Carmen is in the Avenida Mancomunidad; the stop for the Costa Teguise is in Avenida del Generalisimo.

Taxis

Taxis are much in evidence in Lanzarote with taxi ranks in Arrecife, Teguise, Costa Teguise, Puerto del Carmen, Playa Blanca and the airport.

Every taxi driver is required to carry a price list of fares. Price per kilometre is 35 pesetas, with a minimum fare of 200 pesetas (£1.03). Waiting time is charged at 960 pesetas (£4.94) per hour. It is advisable to agree the fare before entering the taxi. Examples of fares are: Airport to Arrecife — 540 pesetas (£2.78); to Puerto del Carmen — 840 pesetas (£4.32); to Costa Teguise — 1300 pesetas (£6.70); to Playa Blanca — 2700 pesetas (£13.90). A four-hour tour of the island costs 6000 pesetas (£30.90), a six-hour tour 7000 pesetas (£36).

You can telephone for a taxi: Airport 81 46 55; Arrecife 81 16 80; Puerto del Carmen 82 50 35 and 82 50 34.

Car hire

Self-drive cars are for hire throughout the tourist resorts in Lanzarote. Some petrol filling stations close on Sundays (and public holidays), therefore it is advisable to fill up on Saturday. If you intend to drive your hire car out to the extensive sandy beaches of Papagayo in the south, where there are no roads but rough tracks, the insurance may not cover you for an accident or damage unless you have a jeep. A deposit of about 8000 pesetas (£41) is sometimes required. Vehicle insurance costs about 500 pesetas (£2.57) depending on the class of vehicle. Passenger personal insurance costs about 250 pesetas (£1.28) per day and covers all occupants. Generally you are required to be over twenty-one years of age and have held a licence for six months. It is not necessary to have an International Driving Permit. Most firms will deliver and collect vehicles. This includes the airport. It may be cheaper and simpler to arrange your car hire with your travel agent in the UK and collect the car at the airport. Avis are one of the firms that will also arrange this.

Car hire firms in Lanzarote include:

Avis Airport. Tel: 81 22 56.
Faycan Puerto del Carmen, Tel: 82 52 77; Playa Blanca, Tel: 51 73 44.
Autos Cabrera Arrecife, Tel: 81 05 39; Playa Blanca, Tel: 51 71 08.
Autos Cabrera Medina Costa Teguise, Tel: 81 35 73; Airport, Tel: 70 01 65.

Costs of hire depend on the size of the vehicle and the hire period. For example (per day):

- Opel Corsa, VW Polo or Fiat Uno
  7 days — 2000 pesetas (£10.30); 3 days — 2200 pesetas (£11.34); 1 day — 2300 pesetas (£11.85).
- Jeep Suzuki
  7 Days — 4000 pesetas (£20.60); 3 days — 4200 pesetas (£21.64); 1 day — 4300 pesetas (£22.16).
- VW Golf, Cabriolet, Opel Ascona 1600
  7 days — 4500 pesetas (£23.19); 3 days — 4700 pesetas (£24.22); 1 day — 5000 pesetas (£25.77).
- Mini Bus 9 seats
  7 days — 5500 pesetas (£28.35); 3 days — 5700 pesetas (£29.38); 1 day — 6000 pesetas (£30.92).

Mopeds, scooters, bicycles

Mopeds, scooters and bicycles are for hire and provide a good way of seeing the country because Lanzarote is fairly flat. The costs quoted below are based on one firm, Moped Montuori in Playa Blanca. Insurance costs 700 pesetas (£3.60), minimum age 16 years. You will need to show your passport and you can pay by Eurocheque or Visa.

- Mopeds
  7 days — 850 pesetas (£4.38); 3 days — 900 pesetas (£4.63); 1 day — 1000 pesetas (£5.15).
- Scooters
  7 days — 1800 pesetas (£9.27); 3 days — 1900 pesetas (£9.79); 1 day — 2000 pesetas (£10.30).
- Bicycles
  7 days — 750 pesetas (£3.86); 3 days — 800 pesetas (£4.12); 1 day — 850 pesetas (£4.38).

Excursions

The most popular coach excursions are the full day island tours, which will include lunch; usually you are picked up from your hotel or apartment at 0830 or 0900 hrs, returning at 1700 to 1800 hrs. On Lanzarote there are two main tours. An excursion to the south takes in Fire Mountain, a camel ride, El Golfo, the salt pans of Salinas de Janubio, Yaiza, Playa Blanca beaches and Puerto del Carmen for shopping. The northern excursion will include a stop at Teguise, the old capital, Haria with its palm trees, the Mirador del Rió, Cuevas de los Verdes, Jameos del Agua (the latter both exciting caves) and possibly a stop for wine tasting. Price is about 5600 pesetas (£28.86), children 2800 pesetas (£14.43).

Canary wrestling

The origin of *lucha Canaria,* this most popular of Canarian sports, goes back to the time of the early inhabitants of these islands, the Guanches. From a very young age village boys gauged their skill and strength with this strenuous game.

Public contests take place between two teams of twelve players; only one member of each team at a time are in the *terrero,* the circular ring of ten metres diameter, which is covered with sand. This being a very sporting game, each member greets the opposite with a handshake *(saludo)* before the contest. Competitors wear short sleeved shirts and rolled up shorts (with another pair underneath); grasping the end of the opponent's shorts is mandatory.

At the start of the contest, the contestants must rest their head on the other's shoulder, one hand on the adversary's shorts and the other touching the ground. The referee blows a whistle and the contest begins. The winner is the first to force any part of the other's body to touch the ground during a timed round. Much excitement is caused when a smaller and more nimble fighter tumbles his heavier opponent.

These *luchadores* become popular local heroes. The matches are events that are attended by families and nowadays *lucha Canaria* is regularly televised.

Teguise

A Sunday morning excursion to the large flea market in the old capital of Teguise, busy with colourful stalls. Price adult 1500 pesetas (£7.73), child 800 pesetas (£4.12).

Lucha Canaria and folk dancing

At Uga, you can see Canary wrestling, local dancers performing and have a barbecue meal in an attractive setting. Cost 3600 pesetas (£18.55), child 1300 pesetas (£6.70).

Jeep Safari

An organised jeep excursion, which goes off the beaten track to see the wilder parts of the island; excellent for photography. Cost about 6000 pesetas (£30.92).

Moonlight Bay
This is an evening out, when you dress up for dinner, dancing and a floorshow in Puerto del Carmen. Cost 4000 pesetas (£20.60).

Sailing ship, 'Marea Errota'
A beautiful old, twenty-five metre ship with sails takes tourists from Arrecife down the coast as far as the beaches of Papagayo. The crew entertain with gymnastics in the rigging. Cost 5000 pesetas (£25.77), child 2500 pesetas (£12.88).

Ship Attoy
This is a cheery family outing from Playa Blanca. You spend the day at sea, sailing along the coast of Lanzarote, with fun, games and a barbecue lunch aboard. Cost 4700 pesetas (£24.22), child 2550 pesetas (£13.14).

Splash Out waterpark
A half-day visit to a water park with plenty of water amusements for the family, also sun beds, bar and restaurant. Cost 2900 pesetas (£14.94), child 1500 pesetas (£7.73).

La Graciosa
A small island at the north west tip of Lanzarote, reached by boat from the port of Orzola which departs at 1015 hrs for a day trip costing 500 pesetas (£2.57). Deserted beaches and small fishing community.

Fuerteventura
A good way to see the north of the neighbouring island of Fuerteventura. You travel by sea and a coach that takes you to the old capital, Betancuria, and the sand dunes by Corralejo. Cost about 6000 pesetas (£30.92)per adult, 3000 pesetas (£15.46)per child.

Las Palmas, Gran Canaria
A one-day excursion by air and coach, to see part of the island and shop in the city of Las Palmas.

Tenerife
Fly to the capital, Santa Cruz, with an excursion to see Mount Teide, Spain's highest mountain, and visit Puerto de la Cruz.

El Aaiun, Morocco
You can fly to this Moroccan village, visit a camel market and have a meal in Africa. A day trip costs 17,000 pesetas (£87.62).

Marrakech, Morocco
An early start is needed for this flight to Morocco, and then by coach to the bazaar of Marrakech. Cost 26,000 pesetas (£134), child 20,000 pesetas (£103).

EIGHT

Lanzarote's restaurants, nightlife and leisure activities

Restaurants

There is a wide choice of restaurants in Lanzarote and the good standard remains similar in all the tourist resorts. There are said to be over one hundred and fifty in Puerto del Carmen. Menus are to be found written in several languages and tend to favour international dishes. These days it is not easy to find genuine Canarian cooking, unless you drive out to the villages. Even there chips seem to be the general order of the day, replacing the tasty *papas arrugas* (small potatoes cooked in their skins in salt water).

With the opening of five-star hotels on the island, à la carte and gourmet dishes of high quality are available at the appropriate price. Because of the high percentage of British tourists in Lanzarote, cafés advertise British breakfasts which are served until noon. Traditional Sunday dinners of roast beef, Yorkshire pudding, two vegetables and roast potatoes are popular. For the families that enjoy ice cream there is a vast choice: you can order enormous dishes often topped with loads of creamy froth and colourful paper parrots or flaming sparklers. Eating hours are earlier in tourist type restaurants, with dinner commencing at 1830 hrs.

Here are some restaurants where we have eaten, or which have been recommended to us.

Arrecife

Cafeteria Avenida Avenida Mancomunidad. One of row of cafés on the promenade, opposite the Arrecife Gran Hotel. You can sit on the terrace and watch the passing scene.

Cafeteria La Tertulia Plaza de la Constitucion. Busy city bar with plain tables and quick service.

Castillo San José in the outskirts of Arrecife. The ideal setting for a romantic meal overlooking the harbour, reasonably priced and good food. Open daily from 1100 to 0100 hrs. Tel: 81 23 21.

The Castillo de San Jose, once an important defence, now houses a modern art gallery and an attractive restaurant overlooking the harbour.

Chino Shiao Avenida Mancomunidad. Opposite Arrecife Gran Hotel. Large restaurant serving mainly Chinese dishes.
El Laurel Calle Almirant Boado Endeiza. High class, large, air-conditioned, polite service, quiet decor.
El Zaguan Calle José Antonio 12. Noted for fish, meat and Canarian dishes.
Las Salinas Snack Bar Calle José Antonio (next to Windsurf Shop). Small simple bar restaurant, used by the locals.
Juan Carlos Calle José Antonio. Opposite Trasmediterranea office. Clean and nice decor, with international menu.
Taiwan Calle Canteljas. Behind Arrecife Gran Hotel. Reasonably priced Chinese restaurant, owned by same people as Chino Shiao on seafront.
El Tronco In the fishing harbour area. A small *tipico* restaurant used by the locals.

Costa Teguise

Copacabana Playa Bastion. Open from 1200 hrs until midnight. Agreeable decor with central fountain, floorshows at weekend.
La Graciosa Hotel Melia las Salinas. For a sophisticated dinner you cannot do better than dine in this luxury restaurant. Open from 1900 hrs until midnight, closed Sunday. Highly recommended.
Los Aljibes At the beginning of urbanisation. Modern restaurant with extensive fish and meat menu, also *paella.* Closed on Wednesday.
Malvasia Grill In Los Zocas complex. Upmarket with international menu, including lobster thermidor, used by visiting notables. Reservations advisable. Open from 1930 until 2230 hrs.
Olas Steak House Playa Bastion. Open at 1000 hrs for breakfast. Snacks and full meals throughout the day until 0300 hrs. Menu of the Day is 800 pesetas (£4.12).
Prado Verde Pleasant and friendly service and cheerful music. International menu.
Tabaiba Pueblo Comercial, near Las Cucharas beach. Elegant with wide menu.
Taipei Chino A friendly Chinese restaurant, suitable for children; good value and quick service.

Puerto del Carmen

Amadeus Piano Bar Restaurant Upper level, near San Antonio Hotel. Open for dinner with quiet piano music.
Bourbon Street Old town. Night spot for dinner and dancing. Open 1830 hrs until very late, seven nights. British band.

Casa Roja By old harbour. Excellent and expensive menu with good service.
El Ancla By church. Quaint, good for fish, pizza and ice cream. English hosts.
El Sardinero By old port. Local menu with fish a speciality.
Kakatoa First floor Fariones Centre. Indonesian and Indian menu.
La Bohème On seafront. Popular, good menu and high prices.
La Bolsa Calle Guanapay. English roast, cheerful.
La Gaviote In San Antonio Hotel. Select, expensive but worth it.
La Marina On seafront. Open for lunch and dinner. Paella, Chateaubriand, fish. Children welcome, good value, closed on Tuesday.
La Ola On seafront with terraces overlooking sea. Pleasant. International menu, expensive but good value.
Pena Mar Beach road. Upstairs, large Indian tandoori restaurant. Open 1800 hrs until late, seven nights.
The Londoner Near San Antonio Hotel. Traditional British style fish and chips. Children's meals and take-away.
Titanic Calle Los Dragos, Avenida de Las Playas. Tel: 51 07 80. Rather up market, modern and overlooking the beach. The Chateaubriand for two at 1100 pesetas (£5.67) is super.
Varadero In converted boathouse by harbour. Very popular, gourmet — you may need a reservation.

Playa Blanca

Brisa Blanca On beach. Good views and international menu.
Casa Pedro Comercial Limones. Spanish, fresh fish and seafoods, open until 2200 hrs. Reasonable and popular.
Casa Salvador By sea front in centre of village. Good fish, long established, Canarian.
El Bistrot Comercial Limones. French style with international menu.
La Bocaina By petrol station. Established, clean. Spanish flambés a speciality. Not cheap.
Los Hervidos Near cross roads in centre of village. Small Canarian restaurant, recommended.
Mama Rossa Comercial Limones. Italian dishes, friendly service.
Tipico Español By church. Spanish, always busy with good service, international menu and *tappas.*

Other restaurants in Lanzarote

Acafife Teguise, near centre of plaza. Old established bar restaurant, moderate prices.

Casa Carlo Playa Honda. Canarian, good fish.
Casa Emiliano Fémes, centre of mountain village. Peaceful atmosphere.
Corjillo Haria, in centre of town. Quiet Canarian, very pleasant.
El Campesino Mozaga. Tourist venue, by César Manrique's monument. Self-service buffet, interesting.
Galeta Near Arrieta, by sea front. Small, simple Canarian, excellent food, prices average.
La Cometa Playa Honda. One of the few vegetarian restaurants. Canarian.
La Galeria Taberna Teguise. Friendly, Canarian cooking, local cheese, reasonable prices.
La Bajas Caleta de Famara. One of the good fish restaurants in this village.
Palacio El Golfo. Round the corner from the El Golfo pool. Simple restaurant with good fish menu.
7 Islas Playa Quemada. Quiet restaurant away from the crowds, specialising in Canarian and fish dishes. Open 1200 to 2200 hrs.
Tiagua On road leading to village. Attractive, small restaurant in old farmhouse, with tiny rooms, local farm tools. Serves goat and rabbit stew, good portions.
Tinajo On road leading to La Santa. Clean, Canarian, international menu, average prices.
Callao Orzola. Large Canarian fish restaurant by the harbour.
Pabellon Mala, just off the Guatiza — Arrieta main road, behind Kleiner Park. German run, upmarket restaurant, open from 1700 to 2300 hrs. Smart decor, your meal cooked at your table on a hot stone, which is then used as your plate. Very appropriate for this island.

Nightlife

Although there is no casino in Lanzarote yet, the nightlife is lively in the tourist resorts. All the big hotels have some entertainments, and many bars and restaurants stay open until early morning. The brightest venue must be **Puerto del Carmen,** where you have a large selection of wine and dine places, sing-a-long pubs and discos. Centro Atlantico is where most of the action takes place, with the Big Apple Disco and Jokers Disco open until 0500 hrs, also Rick's Bar with music and video. The other discos are Bananas and Parking, the latter being a nightclub that is designed to resemble an underground carpark, with car seats to sit on. Winston's Disco is opposite the post office in the old town, and Mavi by the Barcarola complex is a modern disco pub that is open until 0500 hrs.

At the Fariones Hotel, in the Cactus Bar, you can enjoy the Africa Show from Senegal which starts at 2200 hrs. The Hotel San Antonio has music by different groups in the Cocktail Bar. The Beach Club discotheque within the Marina Bay Centre has a luxurious decor and is a popular nightclub. International cabaret entertainment, whilst dining, is offered at Moonlight Bay, upstairs in the Costa Mar Commercial Centre, which was opened by Vince Hill. Entrance costs 1000 pesetas (£5.15) and dinner is from 5800 pesetas (£29.85).

Costa Teguise is fast becoming popular with night owls and the new hotels and apartment blocks offer bright lights and music. The entertainment at the Melia Las Salinas hotel is varied with flamenco, Canarian folk dancers and singers. Inside the Los Zocos Club Resort opposite is Club Aguamarine which features a large glass-domed roof, combined with a modern fantastic light and sound systems. Dancing and live shows are held each evening.

A memorable night out can be had attending a musical concert in the underground caves of Cuevas de los Verdes. Even more colourful is to have dinner and to dance at Jameos del Agua, open three nights a week from 1900 to 0300 hrs. At certain times of the year musical concerts are held. Yehudi Menuhin, the violinist, has praised the acoustics here.

The flat-roofed houses at Uga are reminiscent of North Africa. In the background is the red volcanic Timanfaya Fire Mountain.

Playa Blanca is still in its infancy as a tourist resort, nevertheless it can offer some cheerful entertainment at night. A good choice of restaurants and bars are close at hand, while in the hotels you can enjoy music and dancing. In the Hotel Playa Dorado their Happy Hour is from 2030 to 2200 hrs and the disco is open from 2200 to 0300 hrs.

The Timanfaya restaurant in **Uga** is in an old farmhouse, turned into an attractive restaurant, used by coach excursions. A cheery evening out will include dinner, an exhibition of Canary wrestling *(lucha Canaria)* and Canary folk singing and dancing.

Nightlife in **Arrecife** is limited. There is a cinema which shows mainly Spanish films or films dubbed in Spanish. The Bambi Night Club, behind the Café de Paris, is on Avenida Mancomunidad almost opposite the Arrecife Gran Hotel, open 2000 to 0300 hrs. This is mainly disco music and sometimes a group is featured.

Shopping

Shops on Lanzarote are open at 0900 to 1300 and then from 1600 to 1930 hrs, mornings only on Saturday and closed on Sunday. There is an abundance of supermarkets, some of which are open all week in tourist resorts. Even the smallest village will have a little self-service store where goods are price tagged and there are trolleys and baskets.

Handicraft shops are to be found in all the tourist centres. Hand embroidery, local pottery, costume rag dolls are much in evidence. Big straw hats, as worn by the workers in the fields, and palm woven boxes are on sale. The *timple,* a handmade stringed instrument, manufactured in Teguise at the workshop of Juan Morales, is an unusual purchase. Jewellery and ornaments fashioned from *olivin* (peridot), the semi precious green stone found in the lava rock, are pretty and something different to seek.

Because there are now so many apartments on the island the variety of foodstuffs is wide, with goods being imported from Europe and beyond. Fresh and frozen meat and fish, local and imported fruit and vegetables are widely obtainable and owing to the demands of international visitors the choice is varied. Toilet requisites, medicines, toys and games are to be found in Arrecife and elsewhere. Electrical goods, cameras and watches can be good buys. Alcoholic drinks are certainly cheaper than in the UK, and the same applies to cigarettes and cigars. Lladró porcelain made in Spain, is popular, but make sure that you have an authentic piece if you wish it to be an investment; each genuine figure has a number and flower inscription on its base. If these seem too expensive, then similar porcelain, such as Nao, makes a pleasant ornament at a much lower price.

Buying clothes locally

When in Lanzarote you will be able to purchase holiday clothes in many boutiques, even fashion shops in Arrecife and Puerto del Carmen. The larger hotels have small shops selling quality clothing. Casual and beach wear, as well as sports kits, are now available in some supermarkets. There are a number of shoe shops in Arrecife. Along the main high street, Calle León y Castillo, on the right hand side going north, is a large emporium called Cadena Spinola which has a great range of goods, including clothes. Bargain counters will be marked *rebaja,* which means a reduction in price.

The Canaries being a free market, you may be able to find some bargains in silks and leather goods. Hand-embroidered blouses, skirts and shawls are not easy to find and beware of imports from China and Taiwan.

On Sunday morning, from 0900 to 1300 hrs, there is a craft and flea market at Teguise, where cheap T-shirts and jeans are amongst the variety of goods on the stalls, and there is no shortage of clothes for children.

Souvenirs

In the tourist areas of Costa Teguise, Puerto del Carmen and Playa Blanca you will find a conglomeration of articles designed for souvenir hunters, these range from silver tea spoons to large pieces of pottery. Although many will have a label saying 'Lanzarote' very often they are not made on the island at all. However, Lanzarote's *malvasia* wine is locally produced as is the green *olivina,* which is also known as peridot, a semi-precious stone, which makes attractive jewellery. Quite unusual are colourful tiles depicting island scenes, sometimes they are framed. Gifts made of woven palm leaves are light in weight and the hand embroidery from other Canary islands is easy for packing. There are a number of local artists whose paintings are for sale.

Art galleries and museums

Castillo San Gabriel (Museo Arquelogico) Once this fortress guarded the harbour of Arrecife, now it continues to play an important role as the guardian of archaeological relics of Lanzarote. Ancient fossils, sub aqua finds and Guanche remains, including human bones, are amongst the interesting exhibits. Open from 0900 to 1500 hrs daily. Entrance costs 50 pesetas. There is a large carpark opposite and a good view over the town from the roof.

Castillo San José (Museo de Arte Contemporaneo) This eighteenth-century castle overlooks the harbour, just along the coast from Arrecife. It has been very well restored under the direction of César Manrique, and now houses the International Museum of Contemporary Art, where a permanent collection of modern paintings, sculpture and art forms is kept, including works by César Manrique. Open every day from 1100 to 1900 hrs. Downstairs there is a very pleasant restaurant and bar that closes at 0100 hrs. Tel: 81 23 21.

Museo Sacro de Haria This recently opened, small museum of sacred images is near to the church in the town square.

Casa Museo del Campesino Located almost in the centre of the island, near Mozaga, and close by César Manrique's striking white painted monument, El Campesino, this is the House and Museum of the Agricultural Worker — an old farmhouse, turned into an interesting exhibition of old farm tools and utensils. The restaurant specialises in hot and cold typical dishes; you can try the local wine, too.

Galeria Yaiza You will find this small art gallery on the southern edge of Yaiza, on the road to Playa Blanca. Paintings, ceramics, sculptures and artistic photography by Lanzarote's artists are exhibited. Especially interesting are some old photographs of Arrecife taken some twenty-five years ago. Open from 1700 to 1900 hrs Monday to Saturday.

Palacio de Spinola, Teguise This is a sixteenth-century palace, where some rooms are now open to the public. It also houses an art gallery. Special art exhibitions are sometimes held here.

El Aljibe Art Gallery Part of the Almacén Arts complex in Arrecife, at 26-33 Calle José Betancourt, this art gallery houses works of César Manrique as well as several other Lanzarote artists.

Concerts

Within the Castillo de San José there is a recital room and unusual auditoriums are within the Jameos del Aguas and the Cueva de los Verdes (caves). At these places concerts are held throughout the year, with musicians and artists coming from all over the world to perform. Musical ensembles also give concerts at the Convento San Francisco in Teguise. Tias has a Municipal Theatre. Amongst performances held in this theatre is the Festival of Canarian Music.

Sports

Lanzarote is an island much favoured by sports people, who enjoy the clear air and the variety of sports facilities. In Puerto del Carmen the **Insular Sports Centre** is for tennis, squash and swimming. Open all day, it has restaurant and snack bar, near the sun terraces. **Castellana Sports Club** has gymnasium for weight training, work out programme, aerobics and a sauna for men and women. In the Costa Teguise resort many of the hotels and apartment blocks have a sports programme; also there is a sports club called **La Toca.** At **La Santa,** on the northern coast, a large sports complex has apartments and time share. It has been used for training by the British Olympic Team.

Cycling

Lanzarote is mostly flat and most of the roads are suitable for cycling; in the country there is very little traffic. This is a popular sport with the locals who can be seen in numbers at the weekend. Bicycles can be hired in the resorts and it is possible to bring your own in the aircraft.

Diving

There are facilities for diving at Los Cocoteros, near Guatiza, La Santa and near the old harbour in Puerto del Carmen, where **Clubulanza** is open from 1000 to 1600 hrs. Here experienced divers are welcome, but you will need a temporary membership of the Spanish Diving Club and will be required to verify your qualifications. To speed your application bring your passport with two photo copies of pages two and three, also two photographs.

Fishing

Fishing off the rocks and harbour jetties is popular with the locals as well as visitors. Rods and tackle can be bought from shops in the towns. Some deep sea fishing can be enjoyed but is expensive. Enquire at the old port at Puerto del Carmen or at your hotel.

Football

For Canarians this game comes top of the popularity polls. In

Arrecife the **Club de Bolos** has a football stadium and in every village a space is cleared for a football pitch. Local teams compete in inter island league matches.

Golf

You can enjoy golf at the **Costa Teguise Golf Club,** Campo de Golf, which lies to the north of the resort. This is a unique golf course because it has been made from what was volcanic *malpais* land devastated by past volcanic eruptions. Tons of soil and much hard work has created a green oasis of a nine-hole course, soon to be extended to eighteen holes. An elaborate underground system of watering now keeps the greens in good order. Should you be there early in the morning, you are likely to observe some wild life, such as a pair of Barbary partridge. The club house contains good changing rooms, lockers and showers, open from 0900 to 1830 hrs. A restaurant, pro's shop and the use of electric buggies are among the facilities. Passes are issued to residents and visitors, the latter being charged 4000 pesetas (£20.61) to join the club. Use of greens is by ticket; seven tickets used within twelve days cost 20,00 pesetas (£103); fourteen tickets for use within twenty-five days cost 36,000 pesetas (£185). Hire of full set of clubs, 1800 pesetas (£9.27), half set 1000 pesetas (£5.15).

As the club is sited in an elevated position there are extensive views from the greens towards Arrecife, the harbour and over the Costa Teguise developments. A courtesy bus runs between the Melia Las Salinas Hotel and the Campo de Golf.

Sailing

Because the seas off Lanzarote can be very rough, there is not a lot of off-shore sailing. However, power boats, cruisers and yachts are on the increase, with marinas being developed at Arrecife, Puerto Galero and Playa Blanca. **Club Nautico,** Arrecife is a private sailing club, but a new Marina is nearly complete.

Squash

A number of large hotels have squash courts, and they may be hired from Club Insular in Puerto del Carmen and the Toca Club, Costa Teguise.

Swimming

The warm waters around the coast make swimming in winter possible; however, beware of the winds that whip up suddenly and cause heavy rollers. The safest beach is at Puerto del Carmen, but

Many old tracks provide pleasant walking amongst the volcanic countryside. This one leads towards the Monte Corona crater in the north.

do not swim if the red flag is flying. At Costa Teguise and Playa Blanca some manmade beaches are sheltered by jetties, so children can enjoy the sea. Care must be taken at Papagayo and Playa de Famara, where the undertow can be very strong and dangerous. A pleasant swim can be had at some of the little sandy bays near to Orzola, but sometimes you may find tar on the beach. There are plenty of swimming pools in the hotels and apartment blocks for lazy and safe swimming.

Tennis

Practically all the hotels and some of the apartment blocks have hard tennis courts. You will find professional tennis coaches at the **San Antonio Hotel** in Puerto del Carmen. Usually racquets are for hire at a cost of about 1000 pesetas (£5.15).

Walking

Although Lanzarote does not have good mountains for walking or climbing, and much of the land is rough volcanic lava, yet people are discovering that the island offers some pleasant walks in peaceful scenery. An excellent book, *Landscapes of Lanzarote* (see Bibliography) gives detailed descriptions of walks and picnic areas. We would like to suggest that if you are in the Playa Blanca resort, it is not difficult to walk to reach the Papagayo beaches, and enjoy a dip in the sea before you return; take a drink with you as there is no refreshment en route. You will no doubt need a sunhat as there is no shade anywhere.

At the other end of the island, near the Mirador del Rió, we have enjoyed some wonderful walks along the El Risco de Famara. The views are amazing looking down on the Playa de Famara and La Caleta, while out to sea is the island of La Graciosa. It can be windy and foggy here on the odd day in winter, otherwise it's a lovely spot with plenty of scope for walkers of all capabilities.

It is a unique experience to walk in Lanzarote. Just a word of warning about going on the volcanic rocks or *malpais* (bad land): be careful to use only obvious paths and trails, for the rocks can be loose and quite dangerous — and you can get lost.

Windsurfing

This island is often quoted as being a windsurfing paradise. Every year at all seasons, windsurfers from many different countries come here especially to enjoy their sport. Since it's a small island the enthusiast can easily dash from one part to another to find the most suitable wind on a particular day. The beach at Playa los Pocillos has a **Windsurfing School** from where equipment can be hired for about 1500 pesetas (£7.73). This is a relatively safe beach for beginners. Another safe place for those learning to windsurf is at the inland lagoon at La Santa. For the more experienced, the beaches at Costa Teguise and Caleta de Famara can provide some exciting waves. There are a number of sports shops in the resorts that sell wet suits and other windsurfing gear. **Lagoon Windsurf Tours** (Springfield Road, Horsham, Sussex RH12 2PJ. Tel: 51304) offer package holidays for windsurfers in the Canaries.

Waterski and jetski

You can try your luck at both these exhilarating sports. Cost is about 1500 pesetas (£7.73) for one waterski trip, and 2000 pesetas (£10.30) for a fifteen minute jetski ride. Available at Costa Teguise and Puerto del Carmen beaches.

NINE

Arrecife

The capital city

Arrecife, the port and capital of Lanzarote, with a population of about 30,000, is in the throes of modernisation to cope with the increase of tourist traffic. A system of one-way streets seems to confuse rather than assist the traffic flow. Most roads are narrow and pedestrians walk in the streets where parked cars obstruct. However it is, on the whole, an easy-going place; the frantic blowing of whistles by policemen as tourists commit minor traffic errors is met with good humour from the townsfolk.

Arriving at **Arrecife,** by sea, one looks upon an island of 'brown pimples', small volcanic mountains dotted along the dry brown landscape. **Puerto de los Marmoles** is at the eastern edge of Arrecife. This is the port where ferry ships and large cargo boats dock. Lying further west is Arrecife's main port, where the vast fishing fleet disgorges its huge tonnage of fish. Opposite the fish wharves is a newly-built marina for yachts with moorings, but at the moment it is not completed.

Arrecife is a town of much charm, but it needs to be properly explored and visited several times to absorb its friendly character. The name of the city means 'reef' and you will notice the inland lagoon, **Charcos de San Ginés,** and some offshore islets. Arrecife became the capital only in 1852 — previously the capital was inland, away from the pirates' raids, at Teguise. Until recently there was little in the way of town planning in Arrecife. Now everything is being made tidier. The new seafront with its Parque Municipal, has flower beds and a few small café kiosks, and public telephones. It is here that the bus to Costa Teguise stops. You will find a bus stop for Puerto del Carmen half way along the Avenida Mancomunidad.

City tour 1

Castillo de San Gabriel — Market — Iglesia de San Ginés — Leon y Castillo — Craftmarket — Las Buganvillas — Playa Reducto (3 hour walk)

The original large natural harbour in front of the town is protected by a series of little islets. One, the Islote de los Ingléses, is connected by an old drawbridge to the **Castillo de San Gabriel.** Leonardo Torrani, an Italian architect in the reign of Philip II of Spain, built this sturdy fortress to defend the port from pirates. Two well-preserved old cannons stand outside as a reminder of past aggressive history. Inside the castle is housed the Archeology Museum, full of ancient fossils, sub aqua finds and Guanche relics. Open daily from 0900 to 1500 except Sundays and public holidays. Admission is 50 pesetas (25 pence).

Castillo de San Gabriel, once an important fortress, is now an archaeological museum. Outside two fine cannons are a reminder of past invasions.

Car parking in Arrecife streets is very limited, but there is a large carpark by the Museum Castillo de San Gabriel, for which a small fee is expected by the attendant; in one corner are some toilets. On a clear day the view from the carpark is worth a photograph.

The waterfront from the drawbridge southwards has a pleasant promenade with seats, statues, beds of flowers and colourful pergolas. Along this promenade in the Parque Municipal de Arrecife you will find the **Tourist Office** of Lanzarote (Oficina de Turismo). This is on the sea side of the road, in a low Canarian type building; at present there is no sign outside to indicate that it is the Tourist Office! The English-speaking lady inside will be helpful. Visitors to Lanzarote can use the services of professional guides and interpreters.

Halfway along the seafront on the inland side, to the east of the Castillo in a street called Calle Liebre, you will find the **market.** It seems very small compared with the one in Tenerife, but has daily supplies of fruit and vegetables, some imported. Locally grown onions, potatoes, tomatoes, melons and delicious green peas are reasonably priced. Fresh white goats' cheese is of excellent quality and makes a sustaining mid-day lunch. A small amount of fresh pork is sold in the market. A *carniceria* (butcher) selling a full range of meats and sausages is to be found in the main part of the town. In a separate building is a fresh fish market which has a plentiful selection.

The main street along the front is called Generalisimo Franco; the post office (*correos*) is situated here, open from 0900 to 1300 and 1600 to 1900 hrs, except Saturday afternoon and Sunday. The busiest street is the Leon y Castillo, with one-way traffic, north from the seafront. Banks are to be found there, opening 0900 to 1300 hrs.

The principal church, **Iglesia de San Ginés,** eighteenth century, is dedicated to the island's patron saint. This fine church, after being closed for three years for restoration, has now been rededicated and is open to the public. Its simple white exterior, with a tall bell tower, holds an impressive light interior. Eight stone columns support a splendid carved wood ceiling. The glittering altar piece is set off with a white background and fresh floral displays, which show loving care and devotion. Be sure to visit the side chapel where there is a beautiful display of sacred images, some of which are used for the month long Fiesta de San Ginés.

Walking up **Léon y Castillo,** an assortment of shops will display shoes, clothing, cameras and watches as well as the usual household goods. There is an amusement arcade, antique shops and on the right hand side going north a big store called Spinola Supermarket. It has an escalator going up for toys, games and glassware. If you turn left into Calle Fajardo you will see another branch of this store, but this is just a one-storey quaint little shop, almost like an old-fashioned Woolworth, with an amazing assortment of merchandise, including some splendid wooden models of antique cars. Along the same street is Librearia Fajado, a useful bookshop.

Back in Léon y Castillo, facing towards the sea and opposite the Banco de Santander, you will see a small African market. By the side of the bank you will find Calle General Godeo and along this street is a small **craft market.** Some of the handmade jewellery here would make an original gift.

To locate the best bars and restaurants in Arrecife we suggest you walk along the seafront Avenida de Generalisimo Franco, until you reach the high edifice of the Arrecife Gran Hotel (there are restaurants and cafés here), then turn inland for a block. In this area are several good eating places including a Chinese restaurant. If you wish to eat with the local population you must wait until 1330 hrs when most of the shops and offices close in Arrecife. While in this part of town you may care to visit the shopping centre called Las Buganvillas which houses a variety of small shops on two floors, also a supermarket, ice cream parlour, snack bar and cinema.

Another place to visit is El Almacén, at Calle José Betancourt 26-33, where an old warehouse has been turned into an art gallery and restaurant, designed by César Manrique.

To the west of town by the Arrecife Gran Hotel is a stretch of sand, the **Playa Reducto** rarely used by tourists, although we have seen the occasional motorcaravan parked there. The area seems ripe for development.

City tour 2

Castillo de San José
(15-minute drive, 35-minute walk, mainly level)

Leave from the main carpark by the mighty Castillo de San Gabriel with its fine old drawbridge, and travel eastwards past the taxi rank along by the sea. On the town side of the road you will notice the tall belfry of Iglesia San Ginés, Arrecife's well preserved old church. A little further on is the police station *(policia national),* then the town hall *(ayuntamiento).* Now you go over a small bridge, and on your left is **El Charco,** the inland lagoon that is used these days for small pleasure craft.

The promenade along the waterfront in Arrecife contains many tropical plants and cacti. Near here is the Tourist Office.

Continuing on you will reach the **Puerto de Naos,** which is the main fishing harbour. It is likely that the smell of fish pervades the air for this is Spain's largest sardine port. It is a real sight to watch the unloading of the myriads of silver sardines as they are conveyed by chute out of the ship's hold into huge lorries waiting on the quay — without one slippery sardine landing on the ground!

Huge tuna, shark, cod, grouper and *vieja* also arrive regularly. Much of this fish goes to the nearby canning factories that employ a large labour force of women. Salt from the Salinas de Janubio salt pans is used to preserve quantities of fish.

On the seaside of Puerto de Naos, a long harbour wall offers shelter for yachts and a new marina with full facilities will soon be completed.

Inland from the port is the Hospital Insular, but our tour keeps us by the sea all the time as we wend our way past the canning sheds, ship's chandlers and along the Avenida de Naos. Notice here some disused saltpans and neglected windmills as you go up a short incline to reach your destination, **Castillo de San José,** an eighteenth-century fortress which has recently been restored.

Inside is found the International Contemporary Art Museum, created by César Manrique, open from 1100 to 1900 hrs, admission free. The design is so modern that it is hard to remember that one is really in an ancient fort. Downstairs, a smart high class restaurant has huge windows giving a clear picture of the harbour below. The restaurant (which closes at 0100 hrs) is one of the more expensive on the island, luxuriously laid out with a black leather bar and modern sculpture. The toilets are worth a mention, as they have been made into a veritable garden grotto with trailing plants everywhere! Outside the paved patio and carpark affords good views of ships and the harbours which are floodlit at night.

If you turn left a short way on from the Castillo, you will go down a short unnamed road leading to the main road Carretera de los Mármoles and a Cepsa petrol station. Along Carretera de los Mármoles, leading into Arrecife, there are factories and the most untidy scrubland in all Lanzarote. A ring road allows you to bypass Arrecife if you have no need to visit it.

TEN

Touring Lanzarote

Island tour 1

Arrecife – Aeropuerto de Lanzarote – Playa de Los Pocillos – Puerto del Carmen (a ½-day tour by car, taxi or bus)

Leaving Arrecife by the GC720 going southwest, you will pass the municipal beach of Playa del Reducto, a rather uninteresting stretch of shoreline (at the moment). The main road, Arrecife to Yaiza, is busy with fast traffic. You pass some light industry factories and a petrol station, then two small urbanisations, El Cable and La Concha. Next comes the urbanisation of tightly packed houses called Playa Honda, where the wealthy of Arrecife have their new modern homes; it is a good place to visit if you are looking for a Canarian type restaurant, but the beach is indifferent.

Six kilometres further on, a bypass intersection of the GC720 is signposted to **Aeropuerto de Lanzarote,** as the road swings left towards the sea. Those arriving by air in Lanzarote have a delightful surprise when they reach the airport building; even the most blasé traveller could not fail to be impressed by its unique decor and sheer cleanliness. Again it is the hand of César Manrique which guided the creation of this superb airport lounge. Supported on plain white pillars is a green and white striped canvas awning that stretches the entire area of the roof, so that the effect is like being in a cool tent. Grouped round the pillars on the smoothly tiled floor are attractive green and white low cushioned seats and tables. Let into the ceiling are areas of light under which banks of tropical ferns are placed. Unfortunately this nicely designed airport building is not being maintained very well and it is sad to see the once beautiful plants being neglected and not replaced. However, the bar restaurant looks

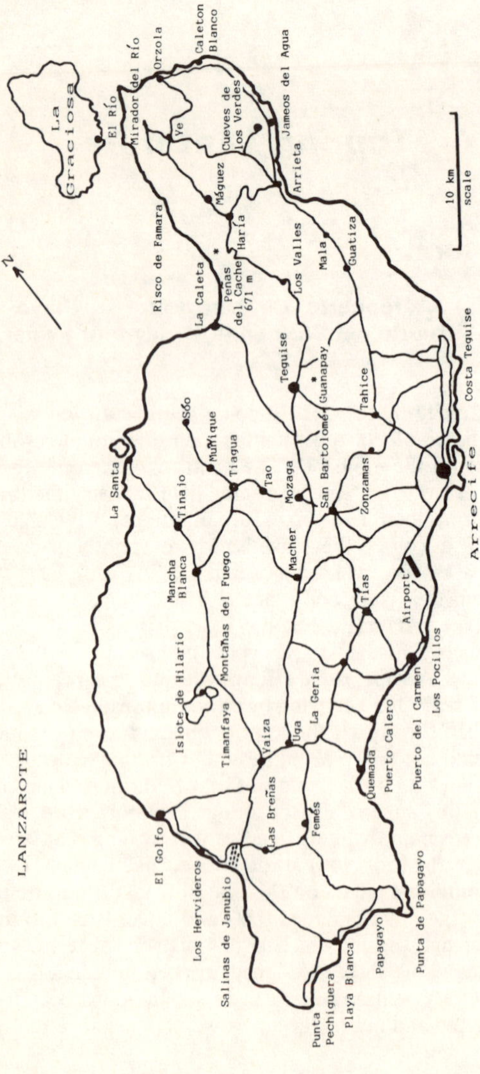
LANZAROTE
N
La Graciosa
El Río
Mirador del Río
Orzola
Caleton Blanco
Ye
Cueves de los Verdes
Jameos del Agua
Arrieta
Máguez
Haría
Risco de Famara
Peñas del Cache 671 m
La Caleta
Los Valles
Mala
Guatiza
10 km scale
Teguise
Guanapay
Costa Teguise
Sóo
Muñique
Tiagua
Tao
Mozaga
San Bartolomé
Tahice
Zonzamas
Arrecife
La Santa
Tinajo
Mancha Blanca
Macher
Montañas del Fuego
Tias
Airport
Islote de Hilario
Timanfaya
Yaiza
Uga
La Geria
Puerto Calero
Puerto del Carmen
Los Pocillos
Quemada
Las Breñas
Femés
El Golfo
Los Hervideros
Salinas de Janubio
Papagayo
Punta de Papagayo
Playa Blanca
Punta Pechiguera

out over the runway and toilet facilities are good. Travel agents, shops, car hire firms and telephones are all on one floor. Taxis, parking and trolleys are outside.

Driving south of the airport by the coast we are now at the beginning of the tourist development **Matagorda,** with hotels, apartments and commercial centres across the road from the sea. This locality is a delightful haven for holidaymakers — well developed with plenty of open spaces, clear water and clean beaches with the near certainty of warm sunshine. **Playa de los Pocillos** is a marvellous wide, golden sand beach, used by families and windsurfers. As you lie on your sunbed you will see aircraft in a low approach to the nearby runway. At the western end of Los Pocillos the four-star Hotel San Antonio always extends a friendly welcome to British visitors.

Opposite this hotel a complex of shops, bars, cafés, restaurant and travel agents provide for a variety of requirements. Nearby villa and apartment accommodation is pleasantly laid out, within easy reach of everything.

Just a short walk from Playa de los Pocillos, along the coast, the road leads into **Puerto del Carmen** (the small port is at the far end). Again this mecca for holidaymakers has a large hotel, the four-star Los Fariones, set close to the sea and providing luxury comforts. Villas and apartments, often with their own swimming pools, gardens full of colour and tropical palms seem to meet every requirement. Numerous shopping arcades, eating establishments, car hire firms and facilities for various sports activities create a relaxed and easy going atmosphere.

Establishments with names like the Bristol Bar, The Victorian Inn with English draught beer, La Pizza, Restaurant Chino, Café Cristina, the Bierkeller indicate what you may expect from them in the way of food and drink. Midday meals are priced around 800 pesetas (£4.08), evening menus start at 1200 pesetas (£6.18). Night clubs, including the Tahiche Club, attached to the Fariones Hotel, are open from 2200 to 0200 hrs, admission is free and on Friday nights there is folk dancing.

Because Puerto del Carmen has been extended up the hill that lies behind the beach, some of the apartments and bungalows can be as much as a fifteen-minute walk away from the sea. The return from the beach could be troublesome for the elderly and handicapped. However, conversely, the very long promenade of six kilometres, makes a delightful walk during the day and at night it is quite romantic.

On the beach sun beds and sun umbrellas make a colourful sight.

The more energetic can hire pedalos, jetskis or enjoy windsurfing. At the western end of Puerto del Carmen is the original harbour and old town, where narrow streets can prove a bottleneck for traffic (a new bypass of Puerto del Carmen is almost complete). You will find the post office and church down near the harbour and this is where to go for the best choice of fish. A flat area by the quay is used as a carpark and coaches off-load holidaymakers who are going on a sea cruise. If you are keen on sea fishing you can use a line here and perhaps catch your supper.

Just above the old harbour, in the Centro Commercial Montana Tropical, Calle Toscan, every Wednesday, a local Arts and Crafts Fair is a lively and cheerful gathering, where you may find some colourful souvenirs.

Island tour 2

Puerto del Carmen – Mácher – Puerto Calero – Playa Quemada – Uga – Yaiza – Salinas de Janubio – Los Hervideros – El Golfo (about a 4-hour drive, with short stops).

The road out of Puerto del Carmen at the western end of town goes up the Calle Juan I, which is lined with shops including one that has 'take away' barbecued chicken *(pollo asado)*. At the end of the developments there are fine views out to sea and the islands of Fuerteventura and Los Lobos. Inland the brown mountain of Montaña Guardilama beckons to all who like to walk amongst the lava fields.

On your way up the hill to Mácher to reach the main highway GC720, you can stop at El Patio and La Finca, which is a combined craft and souvenir shop *(artesania),* and a boutique, garden centre, bodega and restaurant, a good place for last minute shopping to take home. A little further on and you will be at **Mácher,** a spread out village along the main road. This is where the locals live who work in the hotels, restaurants and shops in Puerto del Carmen.

A left turn off the road you have been following from Puerto del Carmen, signposted Uga and Yaiza, undulates past fields and agricultural land. Black lava and *picon* stones cover the ground and a curious system of cultivation, known as *macetas* (flowerpots) is used. Deep holes are dug in the fine black granules and plants such as vines and tomatoes are grown in these depressions, for this *picon* is moisture retaining. Another method of protecting the crops is to

Neat ploughed fields and flat-roofed white houses below a dark volcanic mountain: typical Lanzarote scenery.

make windbreaks of boxes or straw matting. This ingenuity of the Lanzarote farmers is renowned and you might well see a huge field being planted by hand with tiny onion seedlings; the neat pattern of these rows has to be seen to be believed.

If you are interested in sailing and boats then you should make a short detour down to the sea and **Puerto Calero,** where a smart new marina and luxury residences have been constructed. This is a development of high quality with a marina of modern design having every facility. Some very sophisticated yachts are moored here.

Back on the GC720 and on the way to Uga, you notice another road seawards which leads to **Playa Quemada.** Here, at present, you will find only an undeveloped small village, with a beach of stones and pebbles. It becomes sandy at the adjoining Playa de Arena. There are scattered houses and a good fish restaurant — that is all!

Returning up hill to the main route, you may if you are fortunate, see a most unusual sight — a large herd of young camels grazing on the hill above the road. These are cause for passing tourists to stop and get out their cameras and video recorders; rather surprisingly the young animals do not seem to mind this intrusion of snapshot happy tourists disturbing their munching. When fully grown these desert creatures will be used to carry visitors up the side of the Fire Mountain. They are also used to assist with ploughing the fields and at times they are harnessed to the side of a donkey; apparently these two animals are compatible.

Just before reaching Uga a road, left, leads to the mountain village of Femés (see Island tour 3).

The village of **Uga** sits in a little depression of land. White-washed houses and palm trees give it an air of peacefulness. A restaurant and bar called the Timanfaya is a low rambling house with vine covered patio and an outside barbecue. It is sometimes used by coach parties at midday and during the evening; on special occasions folk dancing and music are organised.

Two kilometres further along the main road (GC720) one reaches the town of **Yaiza,** sometimes called the capital of the south. It is reminiscent of North Africa with its low flat-topped white houses and tall palm trees. The spotlessly clean and attractive appearance of Yaiza has earned it awards from the local government and praise for its inhabitants. The central square creates a splendid setting for the large white eighteenth-century church of Los Remedios. Built in 1785, its high belltower stands out strikingly against the clear blue sky. In the square in front of the church decorative lampstands are banked around with cacti and bright flowers, and seats are positioned beneath huge trees for a shady rest.

Walking around this tidy little village is a delight, especially if you are fortunate enough to be there at the quieter moments. It is interesting to note how the villagers accept the hordes of foreigners who peer and stare into every nook and cranny, their cameras always alert for an intimate photograph. These same tourists can enjoy a very good meal at the Restaurant el Volcan. The 'menu of the day' costs 800 pesetas (£4.12). Soup, freshly cooked fish, salad, potatoes, fruit and ice cream, plus bread and wine make a tasty good-value meal and service is prompt and all is clean and friendly. Leaving the cool atmosphere of the restaurant you will probably reach for your sunglasses when you go out into the brilliant sunshine!

A long-established restaurant in the village is La Era, in an old farmhouse built around a courtyard with grain stores and stables serving as dining rooms. It has been decorated with ferns and ceramics and candlelight enhances the picture, while the air is fragrant with mimosa and other sweet smelling plants. An à la carte menu offers a good choice.

In Yaiza you will find a bank, post office and petrol station; on the outskirts towards Playa Blanca is **Yaiza Art Gallery,** which is open only in the evenings.

Continuing westwards beyond Yaiza, one enters a flat area of volcanic *malpais* (bad lands). Except at a spot two kilometres out of Yaiza, where tourist shops and bar restaurants have recently been built, there is total wilderness on both sides of road. Used specially by coach parties, the shops have a good selection of local hand-made gifts so it is a convenient place for souvenir shopping.

As a backcloth to the terrible wasteland, the Fire Mountain, **Timanfaya,** and the volcanic peaks of the National Park can be seen: huge red bronze coloured peaks, deep crevices making dark shadows, the lines and depressions still showing where the lava and earth have been torn asunder.

Six kilometres on from Yaiza the road goes past a large coastal sea lake, the **Salinas de Janubio.** The lake is harvested for salt and has an annual production of 10,000 tons. There is a road down to the entrance where you can view the various processes. To obtain the salt, seawater is pumped into square 'pans', areas where the natural evaporation by sun and wind dries out the moisture. The pumping used formerly to be done by a windmill. After about four weeks the salt is removed and put into piles to dry. The white pyramid shapes of salt make a very unusual picture, as the lake often has a turquoise blue appearance. It is interesting to know that some of the salt is used for the festival of Corpus Christi, every spring, when the local artists dye the salt various colours, then use it to create religious pictures in the streets of Arrecife.

The lake area is a haunt of migrant birds and resident waterfowl so it is popular with ornithologists.

Amongst the birds that are visitors here are white egrets, grey heron, storks, lapwings, plovers and sparrow hawks. This is a pleasant place to have a picnic, you can scramble down to the black sands beach beyond the salt water lagoon, or sit on the cliffs by the Playa Blanca road and watch the changing colour of the light reflection on the salt pans. They can be particularly beautiful in the early evening when the glow of sunset turns the pyramids of salt a delicate shade of pink.

If we continue on the road signposted El Golfo the drive becomes really spectacular, with twists and turns along a shallow clifftop of lava rocks. There are some breathtaking views of eroded lava which juts out to sea, forming amazing holes and caverns where the Atlantic rollers pound the sea into cascades of swirling foam. The sunlight glints and glistens in a rainbow of colour, as wave upon wave crash against the weird shapes, water spilling and splashing in

One of the wonders of Lanzarote is the unfathomable seashore lake at El Golfo.

endless motion. At **Los Hervideros** (Bubbling Spring) steps have been made across the lava rocks so that tourists may clamber down to nearly sea level, to get really close to the gushing waters inside the caves — a fascinating spectacle.

Finally one reaches the end of the road, where a large car park is situated under a huge rock face. From here it is a short walk to visit one of the great wonders of Lanzarote, **El Golfo.**

This is a volcano formed by contact with the sea which produced some rare and beautiful stratifications of different colours and shapes. A lagoon has been formed inside the crater by the infiltration of seawater. Because of microscopic organisms and its unfathomable depth, the lagoon water is bright emerald green, a most unusual sight, making one look twice to believe the colour is not manmade.

All this is set at beach level, so it makes a good place for a picnic. The beach is of pebbles but there are some flat rocky areas. At low tide there is a good view of a natural platform of rock that lies just offshore, looking like a perfect auditorium for performances by mermaids!

Whilst at El Golfo you might like to try your luck at treasure seeking to find some *olivina* (peridot), the green semi-precious stone that lies hidden in the black lava rocks; small pieces have been found on the beach and near the paths. It is likely that a Lanzarote peasant will be about with a simple stall, selling, at a very modest price, chunks of lava with a streak of peridot. Shops in Yaiza and Puerto del Carmen have some jewellery fashioned from this stone which, of course, is quite expensive; but it makes an unusual memento.

Should you feel like some refreshment you can back track up the road from the carpark a short way and take the turning signposted Casas de El Golfo, which involves a drive right amongst the awesome lava rocks until you reach the sea on the other side of El Golfo. **Casa de El Golfo** has some typical Canarian fish restaurants that are now doing good business at lunchtime. Do ask for *papas arrugas,* the little Canary potatoes, cooked with their skins on in salt water. Served with the piquant red *mojo* sauce they are delicious with fresh fish. Should the red *mojo* be too strong for you there is *mojo verde* (green sauce) made with coriander. If you search the supermarkets you can find these Canarian sauces to take home for your friends' approval.

It depends how long you have lingered on this tour whether you have now to return to your hotel; or if you wish you can continue from El Golfo down to the sea at Playa Blanca, as described in the next tour.

Island tour 3

Salinas de Janubio — Las Breñas — Femés — Playa Blanca — Papagayo — (3-4 hours by car; walk from Playa Blanca 1½ hours)

From the Salinas de Janubio, the GC720 towards Playa Blanca passes through an area called El Rubícon, a *malpais* of rather dreary landscape. In 1402 the Normans, led by Jean de Bethancourt and Gadifer de la Salle, reached this southern part of Lanzarote. They set up camp here and named it El Rubicón because of the colour of the soil; it was here that the first Western colony was established and the conquest of the other Canary islands continued. All that remains is the old ruined tower of the Castillo de Rubicón.

Before reaching Playa Blanca you can make a detour. A signposted road to the left is marked Las Breñas. This road climbs quite sharply up to the scattered village of **Las Breñas,** which has a distinct flavour of North Africa, with its white, flat topped houses, all neat and tidy. The small central plaza has a tiny church, while the nearby fields are planted with tidy rows of onions and peas. Looking seawards you have a good view of the white sprawling development that has grown around Playa Blanca. Across the waters lies the tiny island of Los Lobos and the northern shores of Fuerteventura, with the sand dunes of Corralejo.

Above Las Breñas towers the **Atalaya de Femés** (608 m) the highest mountain in the south and part of the Las Ajaches massif. The road winds its way upwards until it reaches Femés which clings to the side of the mountain. Here the church is dedicated to the patron saint of Lanzarote, San Marcial del Rubicón. It was here that the first episcopal seat in the Canaries was established, but the original church was destroyed by English pirates in the sixteenth century. The Fiesta de San Marcial del Rubicón is held every year on 7 July. By the church is a balcony where, on a clear day, you can view an extensive panorama towards the sea. Two restaurants, a bar and an *artesania* shop with a few scattered houses make up the rest of the village. A road going north from Femés winds down an agricultural valley and eventually joins the GC720, quite close to Uga.

There is also a dirt track road south from here that leads down towards the beaches of Papagayo, but we emphasis that this is only passable for those who are using a four-wheel drive jeep, as the road conditions are very rough at present. However, for our tour we will retrace our way safely down from Femés to La Brisa and back to the junction with the GC720, going towards Playa Blanca. This is one of the least attractive drives of the island and the traffic tends to be fast, especially where the road is straight. Looking to the right in the distance you will see a highrise edifice right by the coast. This is the abandoned urbanisation Atlante del Sol, which was never completed. So you are now approaching **Playa Blanca.** On the edge of the resort is a useful petrol station and close by is the restaurant La Bocaina. The main road leads straight down to the sea and the centre of Playa Blanca.

Once just a small fishing port it has now become one of the main tourist resorts of Lanzarote (with Puerto del Carmen as the premier and Costa Teguise in second place). Like all the Canaries the south of the island has a higher sunshine record than the north, hence Playa Blanca's popularity. It is from the port at Playa Blanca that ferries operate daily to Fuerteventura, a sea crossing taking between 20 and 45 minutes, depending whether you use the jetfoil or car ferry. It should be noted that when it is windy this voyage can be rough. Ferry tickets are available at the port and at travel agents nearby. A few fishing boats still use the harbour, which is being improved to provide yacht marina services. Already there is a hoist, water and electric points.

The Alisur Ferry is about to dock at Playa Blanca after crossing from Fuerteventura.

The marvellous wild beach of Papagayo is still unspoilt, without any development nearby.

A new commercial centre, **Los Limones,** has shops, travel agent, bars and restaurants by the sea. Across the road is one of the first urbanisations to be built here, the Wimpey time-share bungalows. Over the last five years further developments have spread westwards, new roads have been built, even manmade beaches have been constructed, and soon this resort will stretch way past Montaña Roja, out to the tall white lighthouse at Punta Pechiguera which is at the southwest tip of Lanzarote.

Close to Los Limones is **Playa Flamingo,** a large development of apartments and villas with a manmade sandy beach. The village has two large supermarkets, several gift shops and a very good selection of restaurants. A small promenade and beach still maintain its pretty fishing village atmosphere. The post office and church are slightly uphill going eastwards, the minor roads leading off are still unmade. At the top of the rise, two four-star hotels are in the luxury class with many indoor and outdoor activities. On the seaside is yet another manmade yellow, sandy beach, and a splendid view of Los Lobos and Fuerteventura.

Most who go to Lanzarote at some time or the other hear about the fabulous beaches of **Papagayo,** and many will find time to visit them. East of Playa Blanca, where new urbanisations are being laid, is a metalled road that follows the coast as far as the **Castillo de las Coloradas,** a well restored castle of circa 1769. After here you need to be a careful driver, for the rest of the route is still, at present, a dusty bumpy track that seems to lead nowhere. In fact there are many branches off it where daredevil jeep drivers have tried to take short cuts. Keep to the main track and look for the primitive road signs for Papagayo; it is a distance of four kilometres or so. Plans are afoot for a tarmac road to reach the beaches. Somehow one feels though that some of the charm of this lovely unspoilt coast will be lost when it becomes so easy to get there.

It is worth noting that there is no shade on the beaches, so it is necessary to have at least a hat and some liquid refreshment; the only facility at present are rubbish bins.

The beaches commence east of Punta Aguila, with Playa de Afe being scruffy and stony. The next beach is Playa Mujeres and then it is El Papagayo. Here sheltered by low cliffs is an expanse of golden sand, bordered with many low growing shrubs, like the spiny *launaea,* with its tiny yellow flowers, also known as aulaga, the camel thorn bush. This is the bush that is fed to the hot cinders at the Islote de Hilario on the Fire Mountain.

Pleasant and satisfying walks can be made along the coastline, though it does involve some scrambling, up and down stoney tracks and across *barrancos,* gorges and sandy banks, so stout footwear is helpful. The sea air is invigorating and the views over the sandy coves rewarding. Playa de Puerto Muelas is referred to as the nudist beach, but naturism is enjoyed on all these *playas.* Some hardy motorcaravanners, too, like to spend a few peaceful nights here, away from it all when the day trippers depart. A moonlight night on Papagayo is something to remember.

Island tour 4

(Timanfaya National Park: about 3 hours)

Timanfaya National Park, situated in the western part of Lanzarote, five kilometres north of Yaiza, must be one of the most extraordinary national parks in the world. Because of the special characteristics of the spectacles to be seen here, and of the geology of the park, visitors are requested to abide by the rules for its use and to follow the instructions of the official guides. The most spectacular and interesting zone of the eruption can be visited by way of the Volcanic Route: there are periodic departures from Islote de Hilario, a restaurant and view-point.

The easiest way to visit **Fire Mountain** is to take a coach excursion. All hotels and apartments will have details of tours in their reception. Should you prefer to drive yourself to the National Park, then your easiest route from Costa Teguise, Arrecife, Puerto del Carmen and Playa Blanca is to go direct to Yaiza. In the centre of the village a sign directs you on to the right road.

At the beginning of the National Park you should notice a metal sign of a little devil with a long tail, holding a fork aloft. This is César Manrique's symbol for Timanfaya, the Fire Devil. The road goes through a vast black wilderness *(malpais)* of lava rock and into view come the colourful slopes of the volcanic cones. Before you reach the entrance barrier to the Volcanic Route you will see on your left a very large car park, where there are toilets and a small bar, discreetly sheltered under the volcanic strata. You must not walk on the black rocks as it is very dangerous, neither must you take any pieces away as a souvenir.

For the more ardent travellers, there are camel rides up the side of the volcanic mountain (about 400 pesetas/£2.06). Two people sit one on either side of a dromedary (always referred to as a camel) in specially constructed wooden chairs. The camels jerk and jog their way slowly to the top of the volcano, their flat feet plodding carefully over the loose ashes. Passengers are not strapped into the chairs, so a sense of balance and strength is required to enjoy the moment! Watch out for the sudden jerk forward as the huge beast gets up off its knees. Once on the move, it is an exhilarating feeling, provided you do not mind the sight of a camel's mouth coming alongside you from behind, its yellow teeth looking dangerously evil. It seems that no one has ever been known to fall off a camel on one of these trips, and practically everyone has a hilarious time. Suspended over the side of a camel on the black cinder slopes of the volcano, with warm sunshine and blue skies above, somehow seems an appropriately unusual way of appreciating the strange attractions of this mysterious landscape with its dark red cones in their silent majesty, motionless and fearfully beautiful.

A short distance on from the camel ride you will come to an entrance barrier and ticket box. It is open every day from 0900 to 1700 hrs, entrance costs 700 pesetas (£3.60), and includes a coach drive from the Islote de Hilaro round the protected area of Timanfaya.

The present area of the park is about 200 sq kms. The range of **Moñtanas del Fuego de Timanfaya** emerged during the great eruptions of 1730 which lasted for six years. This tremendous volcanic activity transformed the physical characteristics of the south of the island, where thirty-two new craters were formed in the midst of a sea of lava and cinders.

This event, considered to be one of the most important in volcanology, had an exceptional eye witness. The priest of the nearby village of Yaiza, Don Andres Lorenzo Curbelo, wrote in his diary the most significant details. He describes the beginning of the eruption as follows, "On the first day of September, between nine and ten at night, the earth suddenly opened up near Timanfaya, two leagues from Yaiza, and an enormous mountain rose from the bosom of the earth, and from its apex shot flames which continued to burn for nineteen days." The eruptions were to continue and destroy whole villages and farmlands for another six years.

Sometimes red, sometimes black, this vast lunar landscape now has roads across it. These roads twist and wind through jagged lava rocks, sinister and black, through a sea of desolation, grim and weird yet with a tremendous grandeur that seems unreal.

Fun for all the family: a ride on a camel in Timanfaya National Park.

The **Islote de Hilario** is a circular restaurant and bar, built out of lava stone which blends unobtrusively with the landscape. It is built on the site of a hut which belonged to an old hermit, Hilario, who (it is said) returned with his donkey after the devastation and planted a fig tree, the only vegetation in the area and an ancestor of the one now growing in the middle of the restaurant.

The volcanos may be quiescent but the inner fires still burn and bubble. At Islote de Hilario impressive demonstrations are given of this phenomenon. Twigs of the *aulaga* bush are dropped into a hole in the ground only 50 centimetres deep; they smoulder and catch fire. Water is poured into a pipe in the lava, and it evaporates immediately and shoots out as a spectacular burst of steam. Ashes scooped up in a shovel become uncomfortably hot when held in the hand. Food in the restaurant is cooked over a specially prepared hole in the ground, a natural charcoal grill. Have a meal cooked by a volcano! A temperature of 400°C is a few metres underground.

From Islote de Hilario tourists can take an hour's bus ride with a taped commentary and music, through the lava to the top of the crater of Timanfaya to get an idea what the surface of the moon is like. It is a fact that the first astronauts were shown photographs of the national Park of Timanfaya to prepare them for their expedition.

It is a truly weird sensation being slowly driven amongst such a devastated landscape. Everywhere are dark, deep crevices and jagged rocks which induce an indescribable sense of shock. You feel overwhelmed by the sheer calamity of it all; but after a while your sense of desolation begins to be replaced by one of admiration for the strange beauty. The colouring and light change at every twist and turn of the way, so that no matter how many times you do the drive always something new catches your eye and you stare with more amazement.

Half way through the drive the coach makes its only stop. You are allowed to alight and walk a short distance to take photographs at a viewpoint. Here you can look down into the centre of craters and right across the volcanic wilderness to the coastline, towards El Golfo.

Because in the last few years there has been some rainfall over Lanzarote, the colour of some of the landscape is altering and this is noticeable on Timanfaya, where patches of lichen are beginning to form on the rocks, and even a few wild flowers are starting to give life on the mountain.

Whether or not you are interested in geology, this ride into the Fire Mountain must surely be long remembered.

An amazing experience on Lanzarote's Fire Mountain: a guide pours a small amount of water into a hole in the ground; this immediately turns into a fierce jet of steam and you realise that the name Fire Mountain is no joke and you are really standing on thermal ground.

Island tour 5

Timanfaya — Mancha Blanca — Tinajo — La Santa — Tiagua — Muñique — Sóo — Tao — Mozaga — San Bartolomé — Zonzamaz Ruins — Costa Teguise (a 3-4 hour drive)

To the east and north of the Timanfaya National Park, in the part known as **La Geria,** the landscape is less harsh but equally novel. This is a comparatively high productive area where vines are grown in little man-made craters of black ash, called *picon,* often sheltered from the winds by low semi-circular stone walls. It is a sight not easily forgotten.

The main road north from Timanfaya passes through **Mancha Blanca** where, so the legend tells us, Our Lady of the Sorrows appeared and commanded the flow of molten lava to stop, thus saving the village from being destroyed. A church was built in the village; it is now the hermitage of Nuestra Señora de los Volcanes, and the scene of an important fiesta each year on 15 September.

Around **Tinajo** tobacco and tomatoes are grown and some green areas are to be seen amongst small farms and villages. Tinajo is a municipal capital, it has a large church, San Roque, whose doors are always open, welcoming visitors to enjoy its sacred treasures, including an impressive carving of the Virgin of Candelaria, the Patron Saint of the Canary Islands. A quiet town, Tinajo has a cinema, petrol station, a few shops and several restaurants.

By continuing through the village to the north you will drop down a short hill across a bare expanse of land to reach the lonely hamlet of **La Santa,** close to the sea. A couple of restaurants here now cater for those tourists who like to get off the beaten track. At the coast is a large, modern highrise complex called Santa Sport. Off shore a small islet called La Isleta has now been blocked off at one end, thereby creating a calm inland waterway. The beach is sandy and both the lagoon and sea are used by windsurfers; the lagoon is safe for beginners but because of strong winds the sea is only for the experienced surfer. Here at La Santa you can enjoy scuba diving, swimming, tennis, basket ball, athletics and play football.

Inside the La Santa building (which is partly time-share) holidaymakers and sports enthusiasts enjoy a vast range of indoor facilities. The British Olympic Team used La Santa for training. For the day trippers this is an interesting place for a picnic and a walk. Take your camera for a colourful picture of the sails of the windsurfers. Sometimes the wind can blow very hard here.

These arenados of black porous lava, seen here in the La Geria region, give protection from the wind to the malvasia grape vines.

Having reached the coast you have to return the way you came, up the hill to Tinajo again. Now look for a turning left, the GC740; you drive past isolated farms and in four kilometres you reach **Tiagua.** On the southern outskirts is a pretty little roadside restaurant. Here you can order tasty Canarian stews of rabbit or goat and sit out on the small patio enjoying the peaceful scene, except when a lorry climbs the hill.

Should you wish to explore further you can take the road north to Muñique and Sóo. This is a lovely country drive, so different to the savage *malpais* lands around the Fire Mountain. Just before you reach **Muñique** you see on the left of the road a very fine windmill. It is worth stopping here to look at this unusual sight of a white plaster duck sitting on the red roof of the windmill.

Across the road you will probably notice in the fields straight lines of vegetables all well sheltered in saucer like depressions of black *picon*. Amongst the rough stony ground, small low lying wild flowers give colour to the landscape. There are fine views, too, over the deserted plain known as El Jable and the distant cliffs of the Riscos de Famara.

Dona Dorotea

Yesterday we went in to the quiet countryside and searched out an old lady called Dorotea, who is ninety years old. She is a famous person in Lanzarote, because she makes ceramics out of local clay, using only her hands, no wheel. Then her pottery is put in the sun to dry, after which it is baked on a wire tray outside, on an open fire burning wood and corn cobs. Because of the wind, the variation of temperature makes each 'firing' different and the pottery very individual. It is a primitive form of art handed down from mother to daughter; one wonders how long this will be done. We had to converse entirely in Spanish, and were able to take some photographs of Dorotea, her daughter and grand-daughter by the fire. They live in a simple cottage down a dusty, rutted lane, away from other abodes, but with a marvellous panorama of sea, cliffs and countryside and the air so clear.

Dorotea makes cooking vessels which can be put in an open oven, though they must be coated with oil before use. Other pottery items include candle holders, hedgehogs, camels and primitive figures of a man and a woman. The reason for these crude figures goes back to a local custom. When a boy wanted to propose to his sweetheart he would present the male figure to her. If she agreed she would then give him a female likeness, as a sign that she wished to be married to him.

This unique pottery is much sought after as each piece is signed by Dorotea.

From Muñique you can drive another five kilometres north to the remote village of **Sóo,** a tiny place with a church and a school, the metalled road ceases just past the village and only a track goes across to **La Caleta de Famara.** Do not try it unless you are on a donkey and have plenty of time!

Having been as far as Sóo you must turn about and return through Muñique to Tiagua, unless you wish to visit the famous potter, Dona Dorotea Armas. Anyone in Muñique will direct you, down a dusty, rutted lane to her primitive shed where she creates her much sought after, handmade pottery.

It is a good road from Tiagua to **Tao,** a pretty village, where in the gardens are growing a spectacular assortment of cacti. Between here and **Mozaga** are the wines whose grapes make the local *malvasia* wine. Situated at the side of the crossroads is a notable monument, La Fecundidad, a statue created in metal by César Manrique, to honour the courage of the peasants of Lanzarote. It is 15 m high and ultra-modern, contrasting sharply with the scenery. What used to be a humble cottage nearby has now been transformed into a museum and restaurant: El Monumento has a courtyard with a *bodega* where you can taste the country wines. In the restaurant, try the local stew, *puchero* — braised goat's meat served with *gofio*. These are rather like dumplings, rolled in a piece of goatskin for shaping before being fried and dunked in stew.

From the Mozaga crossroads you can turn right along the GC730 and the La Geria lava fields. Maybe you will stop at a *bodega* to taste and buy the *malvasia* wine and other souvenirs. This rather poorly surfaced road continues to make its way to Uga and south to Playa Blanca, or east to Puerto del Carmen.

To get to Costa Teguise from Mozaga you continue on the GC740 towards Arrecife. This road bypasses **San Bartolomé,** a

Situated at a cross roads in the centre of the island, this unique metal monument by Cesar Manrique is called La Fecundidao, and is dedicated to the courage of the peasant workers.

municipal town that has narrow winding streets. It also boasts its own folk group, called Aljey, which has been very successful in national and international competitions. The town has its own Fiesta on the 24 August.

From San Bartolemé you can go directly south to the bypass *(circunvalación)* of Arrecife and on to Costa Teguise. or you may drive eastwards, signposted Tahiche, and take a little used road that winds round the brown Monte Mina (444m) in open countryside. As you climb by another volcanic mountain, Montaña de Maneje (228m), look out for the poorly marked site of **Llano de Zonzamas,** the Zonzamaz ruins. They are on the left-hand side coming from San Bartolemé. You will have to park further along the road because of the bend. The ruins are said to be a Guanche fortress and the name comes from Zonzamaz, who was the grandfather of Guadarfra, the last Guanche King of Lanzarote. There is no custodian at the ruins, but the authorities have roofed over part of the dwellings and padlocked the entrance gate. One can just about see inside to the low thick stone walls of the fortress. In the quiet of this low hill you can stand and let your imagination depict the ancient tribe of Guanches, who chose this spot to keep watch against invading marauders.

About three kilometres further along this road you will come to the GC700, main Tahiche to Arrecife road. Just before getting there, look on the left and you will see what was once César Manrique's house, built partially under the lava rock. It is now being made into a museum and the famous artist has moved to Haría. From the crossroads it is just six kilometres to Costa Teguise.

Island tour 6

Costa Teguise — Tahice — Teguise — La Caleta de Famara — Los Valles — Haría — Mirador del Rió (a ½-day drive)

This route for the northern tour starts in Costa Teguise and runs through the spread out village of **Tahice,** passing the oasis of Nazaret, where a number of the pretty villas belong to Europeans.

Soon we see ahead the cluster of mighty buildings of Teguise, once the dignified capital of Lanzarote. During week days this old city is a sleepy place and parking in the side streets is no problem. However, on a Sunday morning you will not get your car anywhere near the centre. From the early morning until 1330 hrs, or later, the **Sunday Craft Market**, also known as the flea market, attracts hundreds of people from all over the island. Both locals and holidaymakers mingle in a cheery crowd amid the many stalls that spread out around the main plaza and into the side streets. Coach excursions to this event are always popular, but be prepared to walk some way. To add to the spectacle, groups of Canarian folk dancers and singers in colourful costume perform in front of the Spinola Palace. This beautiful sixteenth-century mansion has been restored and some of the rooms are open to the public daily, from 1000 to 1300 and 1600 and 1800 hrs. Outside in the plaza two lions, carved in stone, sit guarding the entrance. Notice that one lion looks very fierce to frighten away the pirates and the other one smiles in a welcoming greeting!

High above the plaza rises the great clock and bell tower of the fortress-like Church of San Miguel. Other notable buildings of historic interest in Teguise are the Convents of Santa Domingo and San Francisco and Vera Cruz. The latter houses the crucifix attributed to the famous Canarian carver, Lujan Perez. The Church of Señora de Guadalupe is one of the oldest in the Canary Islands. It is in Teguise that craftsmen make the *timple,* a small guitar like instrument used for all folklore music in the islands.

Two stone lions in the central plaza of Teguise look towards the Palace of Spinola. The fierce lion frightens away pirates; the smiling one welcomes visitors.

The tall bell tower and clock of the mighty San Miguel Church in Teguise is a central landmark. On Sunday mornings a popular market is held in the plaza here.

On the summit of the nearby volcano of **Guanapay,** stands the castle of Santa Bárbara, the oldest fort on the island. Originally a sixteenth-century watch tower against the Moors, it was extended following the attack by the French pirate Francisco el Clerigo. From the castle there are fine panoramic views across the island, even to Fuerteventura on a clear day.

A detour can be made from Teguise to the coast by leaving Teguise on the road for Mozaga and, at 4 km, taking the right turning towards the coast where there is the small fishing village of **La Caleta** and, to the right of the bay, **Playa Famara.** A modern *urbanización* set below a large cliff has the use of the sandy beach. In the village little has been done to destroy its native simplicity. Several simple bar-restaurants provide inexpensive fish meals in local surroundings. At the western end of the village an unspoilt beach of sand dunes and rocks remains little frequented and a small development at the extreme end has not spoiled the tranquillity.

Underneath the massive high cliffs of Riscos de Famara, in the Bay of Famara, rather pathetically, lies the remains of a shipwreck, the upper part still showing above water. It is said to have contained cement and was swept ashore in a fierce gale. It is well to remember that at times this coast experiences large Atlantic rollers, causing a very strong undercurrent, making it dangerous for swimming.

Returning to Teguise and following the road signposted Haría towards the northern tip of the island, one reaches the agricultural area of **Los Valles.** Scattered homesteads and dwellings give the countryside a very peaceful air. It is interesting to see that in some places because of lack of rich soil the vines are grafted into the rootstock of the prickly pear, a moisture retaining plant.

Los Valles is noteworthy because it is here that the people from the south, whose villages were destroyed by the Timanfaya volcanic eruption, were resettled. Their tenacity in struggling against the elements of fire and water to recreate a form of agriculture and way of life against all odds, is an admirable example of man's love for his homeland.

After you leave Los Valles and start climbing, look out for a signpost on the left to Las Nieves, this side road leads to the Ermita de la Nieves (Chapel of the Snows), a solitary hermitage set high on the cliffs, said to be the coldest place in Lanzarote. Here you are close to **Peñas del Chache** (671m), the highest point in island. You will locate this by the communication aerials and domes. Hopefully you will have a nice warm and sunny day, as a walk along the cliffs here is a stunning experience. The views are immense as you look down towards La Caleta way below, and out to sea to the offshore islands of Montana Clara and Alegranza. Perhaps you will also meet the tame raven that like to be fed. It will almost feed from your hand before it flies off to nest in the rock face.

The road to **Haría** winds in a mountainous spiral. At the summit it is surprising to find that the land continues to be terraced and cultivated. Young onions are growing in neatly laid out rows. Maybe you will see the seedlings being planted by hand — a laborious task. No wonder that the farmer may stop to stare and at the same time eat a few of the onion seedlings! The geometrical patterns made by these tidy fields are a noticeable feature of the island.

Two bar-restaurants have been recently built on separate belvederes, affording splendid views northwards overlooking the valley below and the town of Haría, set amid many palm trees. The bars are used by coach tours, and they make a useful parking place, having toilets and small souvenir shops. Haría, amid some of the most fertile fields in Lanzarote, has a picturesque setting. Wild flowers and grass grow along the valley roads and neat white houses, bright with geraniums, bougainvillea, palm and eucalyptus trees, make a colourful picture. This area is sometimes called The Valley of Thousand Palms. There is a legend that says that each palm tree was planted to celebrate the birth of a girl.

In the centre of Haría is a quiet plaza with huge eucalyptus trees and a church. Close by is the Museo Sacro de Haría which contains religious relics. It is open from 1100 to 1300 hrs.

From Haría continue north and in three kilometres you pass through Máguez and when near to Ye you see a signpost on the left for Mirador del Río. On your right you will notice the deep crater of Monte Corona (609m).

Approaching the extreme north tip of the island, the land again becomes bare and dry with only the odd cactus and cardon growing. It is worth remembering that cacti have very small needles that can cause much discomfort under the skin. Likewise the candelabra-like cardon (a tall spiky column cactus) if broken will give a copious discharge of milk sap which is very sticky, so protect your eyes and clothes.

A tall headland, the **Riscos de Famara,** stands out proudly, the basalt rock having sharp points. This site was the Bateria del Rio (battery) built in the sixteenth century as a defence against pirate ships. Today a cleverly designed restaurant and glassed in look-out point built into the rockface enable visitors to enjoy an outstanding panoramic view. The **Mirador del Río** is another of César

Manrique's inspired tourist attractions. Admission is 300 pesetas (£1.54). Open from 1100 to 1900 hrs.

The exterior of the restaurant is entirely covered with lava rock, but inside all is white and green (the Lanzarote motif colours) with white-washed walls, and enormous baskets of *elechos* (ferns) hanging down in cascades of cool green. A narrow balcony just a couple of metres wide, on the far side of the restaurant, allows anyone with a good head for heights to stand right at the edge of a precipice. Down below is the narrow channel of sea called **El Río** which flows between Lanzarote and Isla Graciosa. Most days the smaller islands of Roque del Oeste, Roque del Este, Montaña Clara and Alegranza can be clearly seen. On the beach some salt pans have a strange red glow, while across the water on Graciosa the pure white sands beckon invitingly.

At the bar in the Mirador there is a good selection of drinks and *tappas.* Try some *queso blanco* (goat's cheese) with a glass of cool white wine, then perhaps a portion of delicious creamy gateau decorated with chocolate or fruits. Upstairs above the bar is a small shop selling a few local handicrafts. In the true Manrique style of not being flamboyant there is no sign to show you the way, you have to seek it out!

While at the Mirador you have the opportunity to picnic and walk in some stunning scenery, the air so clear and intoxicating. One is very much aware of the sea and sky. This little island in the Atlantic is very beautiful and up here it is unspoilt and peaceful.

Island tour 7

Mirador del Rio – Orzola – Cuevas de los Verdes – Jameos del Agua – Arrieta – Mala – Guatiza – Costa Teguise (a ½-day drive)

Leaving the Mirador del Río on the main road GC710, you pass through the village of **Ye,** which is renowned for its excellent vineyards. In earlier years the purple dye from the cactus beetle was gathered here from the abundant prickly pear cactus *(opuntia).* The route twists and turns, often with no edge to the road, but there are splendid views of Montaña Corona as you drive south.

Six kilometres from the Mirador del Río, a turning left goes to **Orzola,** a tiny port on the coast. This quiet fishing village off the main tourist route has a beach and several bars. Bar Restaurant el

Callao and Restaurant los Roques both serve excellent fish meals at reasonable prices.

La Graciosa

This attractive island, which is seen clearly from the view point Mirador del Río in the north of Lanzarote, can be reached by taking a boat trip from nearby Orzola

La Graciosa is tiny, only nine kilometres long and four kilometres wide. The peaks of old volcanoes darken its centre but the coast line is mostly made up of lovely white sandy beaches. The eight hundred inhabitants are mainly fisher folk and used to living a very simple life though now, with the advent of tourism and, more recently, of electricity in their homes, the lives of the people of Graciosa are changing. Each year brings more and more visitors across on the ferry from Orzola, and by private boats (price by agreement). Although the distance across to Graciosa is only about a kilometre at the narrowest point, when the wind blows fiercely the crossing cannot be made.

The main town is Caleta del Sebo, with a smaller settlement, Caleta de Pedro Barba, to the northeast; in the former there are two hostels and two bar restaurants, no doubt more will come. It is an ideal place for snorkelling with lots of fish about.

It is possible to walk around the island and visit the isolated beach of Playa de las Conchas, but there is no shade. A nice legend tells that a British ship laden with treasure was ship-wrecked here and the crew buried the treasure in the sands. The ship's cabin boy escaped to England, but died before the exact location of the treasure was revealed. So La Graciosa is said to be a Treasure Island ....

From Orzola it is sometimes possible to take a boat over to the island of La Graciosa. This has to be arranged through a travel agent or at Orzola. The cost is 900 pesetas (£4.63) return but the trip depends very much on the weather and the inclination of the local fishermen. La Graciosa (42 sq km) has a population of 800, who mostly live in the village of **Caleta del Sebo.** There are some lovely bathing beaches there, and talk of further development for tourists. The other small islands are uninhabited.

From Orzola you follow the coastline south past some attractive, white sandy coves suitable for a swim or picnic, called Charca de la Laia, Caletón Blanco and Caleta del Mojón Blanco. These are at the edge of the volcanic Malpais de la Corona, which was just a vast 'badlands', but with the slight increased rainfall of recent years, cardon cactus, euphorbea, tabai, senecio and other low lying plants are appearing here. Some shrub tobacco has been planted too, and gradually the landscape is taking on a pleasant green tinge.

Cuevas de los Verdes is in the area of ancient volcanic activity, twelve kilometres south of the Mirador del Río. Again due to Manrique's dislike of blatant signs, you will have to look hard for the entrance to the caves, for very little is seen from above the ground. Look for a sign showing the 'devil of Timanfaya' — a weird face carved on a piece of pinewood. Thousands of years ago during the Corona volcano eruption, a stream of molten lava solidified into a tunnel, the lava outside cooling more quickly than the central flow, thus creating these caves that were used by the Guanches as a refuge from marauding pirates. Today there is a series of caves six kilometres long, with several more galleries not yet fully opened. Some are under the sea and are of great geological interest. Guided tours and coach parties are shown some of the wonders of these subterranean passages. Open from 1100 to 1800 hrs, admission 500 pesetas (£2.57). The visit takes about half an hour, and it is an eerie experience to go single file along these dimly lit and often narrow passages; in places it is necessary to stoop low to pass into a larger cavern. At one place called El Refugio (where the Guanches lived) a small auditorium has been created, and concealed lighting used to good effect. Remember to wear flat shoes, and put on dark glasses as you come out of the cave, for the glare of the sunshine can be blinding — and mind your head!

Not far away, nearer the sea, in another part of the caves network created by the Corona eruption, is the **Grotto Jameos del Agua,** a natural phenomenon and now one of Lanzarote's main tourist attractions. The combined forces of nature and the clever, loving hand of mankind have achieved a fairylike 'Aladdin's Cave'. Down a short flight of winding steps is a grotto, the sides of which are still in their natural state. Using lava stones a bar has been built: wooden tables and chairs are set amid huge cactus plants and hanging ferns while bright flowers add colour and softness, and subdued lighting gives depth.

Walking further into the cavern and down more steps, one reaches the floor of the cave where there is a shallow pool of seawater inhabited by strange little white and almost blind crabs. These minute creatures are *munidopsis poliforma,* said to be unique in the underwater world. They are easily seen, looking like white stars glistening in the clear water or clinging to the rocks around the pool.

Across a narrow bridge beside the pool are more tables and chairs and another bar, even a discreet toilet tucked away amongst the rocks and plants. Up a flight of steps, daylight can be seen. An inviting swimming pool is available for anyone wanting a cool dip, but only glamorous bikini-clad young ladies seem to dare venture

Where shall we go to next on this peaceful island with its fantastic views? Here at Riscos de Famara a tame raven delights in scraps from a picnic.

into the blue waters! All around the flora is of the most luxuriant variety and little rock pools are inhabited by turtles and ornamental fish, birds twitter and sing as they fly from one cavern to another.

Touring this singular attraction it is hard to believe that it is also a successful restaurant and night club. Twice a week the romantic cave is the scene of a stunning show of folk dancing and changing light patterns on the rocky lava walls and shining waters. It is said that Yehudi Menuhin has played his violin in the cave and found the acoustics perfect. The word *Jameos* means aperture and *Agua* is water, hence the name Jameos del Agua. Do not forget to take a coat and a camera. Men are required to wear a tie and jacket in the evening.

Continue along the coast road to **Punta Mujeres** where abandoned saltpans lie. The name means 'women's point' and it is said this is where the women of the village gathered to watch for pirates and warn their men folk working with the salt.

Journeying southwards one leaves the area of lava rocks behind. On the coast **Arrieta** is fast getting a reputation with tourists as a place for excellent fresh fish meals. **Playa de la Garita** is still mostly deserted and a candidate for development.

Reaching **Mala** and **Guatiza,** fields of prickly pears are seen, grown especially for the cochineal industry. It is in Lanzarote that the cochineal insect is cultivated. The species bred expressly for the dye is the *cocus cactu,* which lives on succulents like nopal. The farmer makes sure that the insects are suitably spread out amongst the plants where the female, almost unmoving on the plant, sucks up the juices of the cactus leaf. After three months the insects have reached full size and can be harvested. They are carefully scraped off the leaves and put in a box to kill them and shake off impurities. Afterwards they are dried in the sun prior to being packed in sacks for export. As a non-toxic substance, cochineal is used for colouring lipsticks, toothpaste and drinks like Campari. In the past this dye has been used for colouring woollen rugs.

On the northern outskirts of Guatiza a large **Cactus Garden**, designed by César Manrique, is an unusual tourist attraction. You will easily locate it by the windmill atop a volcanic mound. At the entrance is another feature — a giant cactus made out of discarded pieces of metal and iron tubes painted green. From a distance it looks real: a typical Manrique creation.

South of Guatiza is a small urbanisation called Los Cocoteros, which specialises in sports holidays. About seven kilometres on from Guatiza you reach the noticeable archway entrance to the Costa Teguise holiday resort.

Costa Teguise is being made with the careful artistic direction of César Manrique. A complex of apartments and studios, in the light and airy Lanzarote style, is set amongst lawns, gardens and swimming pools. Grouped in a typical village manner around a plaza are bungalows offering a more 'community' type of life style. The development includes supermarkets, bars and restaurants. Properties are available to rent or purchase. A further amenity is the 9-hole **Costa Teguise Golf** Course. Passes are issued to Lanzarote residents and to visitors for periods of one month, one week or a day.

One of the first buildings in the Costa Teguise development was the Las Salinas Hotel (originally the Sheraton). Designed to complement the local scenery, this five-star hotel is the epitome of luxury and comfort. The whole appearance is of a green oasis in a lava field. Outside are tall palm trees, tropical gardens, and a large swimming pool looking like a lake; balconies dripping with scarlet geraniums and bougainvillea blend with the white cantilevered building.

The cool marble hall is delightfully restful. Inside a large water garden is open to the skies and banks of tall grasses, ferns and shrubs grow in profusion. Huge green plants trail from containers suspended from the three floors that surround the garden and pool; waterfalls, creating a feeling of opulence in such a dry island, are enhanced at night by subtle coloured lighting. The Melia Las Salinas Hotel has now been somewhat obscured by buildings on either side and at the back. Nevertheless this excellent hotel offers every comfort with friendly and polite service.

Close to the hotel, **Playa de los Charcos** is a small sandy beach. If you are up early in the morning, you may be able to observe a family of Barbary partridge scurrying about for their early morning feed. Another bird to be seen in Lanzarote is the hoopoe, its bright pink, black and white striped plumage and noticeable erectile crest, make it easy to identify even without the characteristic deep 'hoo poo poo'.

Behind the beach there is a large time-share development, which means that you are likely to be approached by touts who wish you to invest in the property. There has been much discussion and publicity about the rate of development at Costa Teguise. It would appear that César Manrique's high ideal of keeping to a low density urbanisation has been overridden. Now the apartment blocks and commercial centres have spread like mushrooms, with more to come. But it must be said that previously this place was only ugly waste land. Now Costa Teguise is a pleasant and mostly quiet holiday resort. Being positioned slightly north of half way along the coast, it is a very good base for touring Lanzarote.

ELEVEN

Introducing Fuerteventura

Fuerteventura is the second largest island in the Canary archipelago, and is, relatively, the least populated, with about 30,000 inhabitants to its area of 2020 sq km — half of whom live in Puerto del Rosario, the capital and main port.

North Africa is only about 90 km away and, indeed, Fuerteventura is very different from all the other islands, because of its desert-like quality, looking and smelling much more like Morocco than Spain. A small mountain range runs down the middle north to south, its highest peak, **Pico de la Zarza** (807 m) in the southern peninsula of Jandía. This lack of high mountains accounts for the low rainfall and is the reason why winds in Fuerteventura can be strong at times, full of dust from Africa.

Island of Solitude

Fuerteventura is known as the Isla de Soledad (Island of Solitude). The great beauty of the island lies in its bare landscapes, with a shore line that includes vast white beaches, practically deserted, and extensive areas of sand dunes. The island is volcanic in origin, full of extinct volcanic cones, wide valleys and bare plains. Small villages with flat topped houses are scattered widely, like green oases: just a few palm trees, a church, several bars and a small supermarket. Windmills draw a small amount of water from the subsoil and tomatoes, lettuce and some cereal crops are grown in the dry volcanic soil. Recently there has been an increase in the cultivation of tomatoes and at Gran Tarajal, in the south, a small boat runs a regular cargo of tomatoes to Las Palmas. The uncultivated land is grazed by goats. Although there are plenty of fish off the African coast the island has only a small fishing fleet, owing to its poor economic state.

Windmills

Because of the lack of water and the need to grind corn, the use of windmills in Fuerteventura has been widespread. Two types of windmill are used. The Molina is a wooden mill that is built on to the roof top of a house, whereas the Molino stands on the ground on struts made of wood or metal. A good example of both a Molina and a Molino can be seen on the La Oliva to Lajares road, near the church, just before entering Lajares. Both types of mill are used to draw water and to grind corn. The country folk use the ground flour to make *golfio,* which they cook in soup and stews, forming part of their staple diet.

In a guide book issued free from the Cabildo Insular de Fuerteventura a windmill route is suggested for the enjoyment of visitors. The main areas to visit are Antigua, Corralejo, El Cotilla, Lajares, Llanos de la Concepción, Tefia, Tiscamanita, Tuinje and Villaverde. It is interesting to note the different types of sails used. All these windmills make attractive photographs.

However, it seems that tourism is going to be the answer to increasing prosperity. Since the building of its new airport, **Los Estancos,** south of Puerto del Rosario, Fuerteventura has been developing tourism. In the extreme north and south a few large hotels and apartments have been built and package tour holiday-makers are beginning to discover the delights of this unusual island.

It is now possible to tour the whole of Fuerteventura on reasonably good roads; only the more remote places still rely on sandy tracks across uneven scrubland. With little traffic on the roads, the main consideration has to be for the stray goats that always have priority of way in Fuerteventura — that is one of the characteristics that make the island so appealing!

History of Fuerteventura

According to many geologists and to the people of Fuerteventura, the island is the oldest in the archipelago. They say it was the result of intense volcanic activity some twelve million years ago. Like all the other islands, the origins of its early people, the Guanches, are subject for discussion. In Fuerteventura some ethnic relationships with the Berbers of North Africa and the discovery of Berber inscriptions lead one to think that the Berbers must have been the original population. Another reason for this theory is that the herding and cultivation methods have a similarity, and there is common use of such names as Baifo, Tofio and Tejuete.

The early inhabitants gave the name Herbana to the island, alluding to the thick vegetation found there (surely they must have had a higher rainfall then than now?) Nowadays the island is almost devoid of trees, except for the planted palms and desert like species such as the euphorbia, the tabaiba and the cardon cactus.

Fuerteventura had already been mapped when early in the fifteenth century the Frenchmen Jean de Bethancourt and Godifer de la Salle set about conquering the island. They eventually subdued the two ruling tribes of Maxorata and Jandía. The two kings, whose names were Guize and Ayoze, were baptised and adopted the names of Luis and Alfonso. They settled in the valley of Betancuria and in 1414 a monastery was built and Christianity came to Fuerteventura. It was then that Bethancourt's chaplains gave the island a name, Forte Aventure.

For a period, the island belonged to the domain of the Lords of La Gomera, finally becoming Spanish National territory in 1496,

Two windmills stand on either side of the Lajares to La Oliva road. The left hand one grinds corn. The one attached to the house draws water.

with the conquest of Tenerife. Throughout the centuries Fuerteventura suffered terribly from raids by Algerian and Moorish pirates. At one time the Moors established their own communities on the island. Their influence can still be seen in the low square whitewashed houses and in some of the domed churches. These adversities helped to form the temperament of the people, who remain patient and reserved, in a land of solitary and monotonous living yet with a beauty of its own.

In the nineteenth century Fuerteventura was incorporated into the Spanish Province of the Canaries. In 1927, by Royal decree the Canary Archipelago was divided into two provinces, with the capital for the western islands in Santa Cruz de Tenerife and the capital for the eastern islands in Las Palmas de Gran Canaria. So today Fuerteventura is in the Province of Las Palmas. Local administration of the island comes under six different municipalities.

The **Majoreros** (the people of Fuerteventura) have always been a hard working and rather reticent people; the harshness of the land has made them strong and independent. Only with the recent advent of tourism have the islanders become more aware of the outside world. Now, with some reluctance, they accept the necessity to develop their island, realising the promise of prosperity to meet the needs of modern Fuerteventura.

Climate

Temperatures never exceed 26°C in summer and do not fall below 15°C in winter. The sea temperature remains constant at a comfortable 20°C all year. No Fuerteventura peasant is seen working in the fields without a straw hat with a large brim, reminding us that the sun's rays in Fuerteventura can be as much as 15 per cent stronger than on mainland Spain, so some protection is required initially, especially if one enjoys the pleasures of naturism, for which Fuerteventura beaches are so suitable.

Rainfall is very low and the island tends to be windy. Of recent years, however, a general increase of rain over all the Canary archipelago has meant that the water situation in Fuerteventura has improved, helped considerably by new desalination plants. The result of this extra moisture is that the landscape has become less arid, and in early spring wild flowers appear. Mountain slopes and volcanic scree are becoming less desertlike, even green. Nevertheless, Fuerteventura is still an island that suffers from strong winds, and the *sirocco,* a hot dusty wind blowing from the Sahara desert, can be humid and unpleasant. Fortunately this usually lasts only a few days, then the air freshens and one sees the sun again.

In the south of the island, the east side of the Jandia peninsula is called *Sotavento* (quiet wind) while the west coast is the *Barlovento* (noisy wind). This also means that the west coast has rougher seas and can be cooler.

What to wear

Lightweight clothes of the drip-dry variety are required. Some of the large hotels have laundry services, but do not expect launderettes if you are in an apartment. Beachwear is not allowed in dining rooms, although in the evenings dress is casual or trendy rather than formal. Take a windcheater jacket; you may decide to hire a jeep type car to tour the island, and winds can spring up quickly and become strong. There are very few clothes shops, but you will find boutiques where the big hotels are situated.

Places of special interest

Some of the places of special interest on Fuerteventura are listed here. They are described more fully in the island tours (Chapter 14). Approximate distances are given from the capital, Puerto del Rosario.

Betancuria (28 km) Ancient island capital hidden away in lovely valley in western mountains. A national historic monument. Seventeenth century cathedral. Small village bar restaurant, souvenir shop, small ethnographic museum.

Caleta de Fustes (13 km) Modern development on east coast, sandy beach, yacht harbour, apartments, sports facilities. Isolated.

Corralejo (38 km) Important town on north coast. Ferry to Lanzarote. Pleasure and fishing boats, yacht harbour. Hotel, apartments, supermarket, shops, petrol, taxis, disco, restaurants. Nearby sandy bay, good underwater swimming, windsurfing.

El Cotillo (39 km) Remote north-west coast fishing village. Tourist development, sandy bays, rocks, good fishing, fish restaurant.

Gran Tarajal (48 km) Second largest town and port. Grey sandy beach. Promenade, shops, restaurants, bars. Petrol, post office, banks.

Isla de los Lobos (38 km to Corralejo) Small islet (2.5 sq kms) north east of Fuerteventura. Day trips from Corralejo. Sandy beaches, swimming, restaurant. Peaceful.

La Oliva (24 km) Quiet historic inland town. Large parish church. Casa de los Coroneles, former governor's palace, now being restored. Casa del Capellan, old mansion, high wooden doors with Aztec design. Post office, shop restaurants.

Las Playitas (51 km) Small developing seaside village, sandy bay and pebble beach, fishing boats, bar and restaurant. Attractive position 4 kms from Gran Tarajal.

Morro del Jable (100 km) Large village in extreme south of Jandia. Fishing boats, fish restaurant, shops, petrol, banks, supermarkets. Hotels at Playa Jandia. New harbour. Jetfoil service to Gran Canaria and Tenerife.

Pájara (43 km) Inland town with notable sixteenth century church with carved stone portal, Aztec design. Peaceful country setting.

Parque Natural de las Dunas (28 km) Amazingly beautiful area of sand dunes on north-east coast. Wildlife, picnics, swimming, clear seas, naturist sunbathing. Hotels at northern end.

Playa Jandía (75 km) Southern peninsula of white sands and flat beaches. Scattered modern developments south of Costa Calma. Splendid swimming, clear seas, sunbathing. Panoramic views, utterly peaceful, naturist area.

Puerto del Rosario Capital town and port. Quietly interesting. Post office, banks, shops, market, small restaurant, petrol, repairs. Headquarters of Spanish Foreign Legion. Nearby Playa Blanca beach undeveloped.

Beaches

Fuerteventura has more kilometres of golden sands than any of the other Canary islands, and these beaches are the main tourist attraction. Altogether there are some 152 beaches, with a total length of more than 50kms of sand (this figure includes the Isla de Lobos). Of course not all these beaches are accessible to the average tourist; you need to be an experienced walker to reach some of them, which are to be found down goat tracks and at the foot of steep cliffs.

To reach this beach at Jandia you must drive down a rough track; beware of soft sand.

Jandia It is acknowledged that Playa de Sotavento, in the south, is the finest of all the *playas*. This is a vast paradise of sea and sands which, despite the recent development of tourist accommodation close to the sea, is still unspoilt and peaceful, and much favoured by naturists.

Las Dunas In the north, from Corralejo southwards, an enormous stretch of white sands has been created a Nature Reserve. Las Dunas, as this area is called, is a natural formation of dunes and beaches, which are continually changing because they are the result of sand being blown by the strong winds from the Sahara. It's a splendid place to get tanned, but do take precautions against the fierce sun as there is no shade anywhere.

Other beaches that can be reached by car

Caleta de Fuste South of Puerto del Rosario and the airport is this partially natural and manmade bay of golden sands. Shallow waters at the edge make it safe for young children. Nearby are toilets, bars, restaurants and shops.

El Cotillo An unspoilt fishing village on the northwest coast, with white sands on both sides. To the north the beach has a series of pretty little rock and sand bays with shallow turquoise water, but no facilities. The other side of the village, past the Castillo a rough track leads along a headland of shallow cliffs, below which are sandy *playas;* sometimes the Atlantic rollers can be very rough here.
Gran Tarajal You must drive into the centre of Gran Tarajal to reach the beach, which has rather uninteresting, greyish sand. There's quite a nice walk along the promenade to the harbour and quay.
Las Playitas Two kilometres before reaching Gran Tarajal, a turning to the left is signposted Las Playitas. This road winds round a hill towards the sea. Just before you enter the village you will notice a track on the right and in the distance a beach of greyish sand, which sweeps round to join the village where the shore is rocky.
Playa Blanca Two kilometres south of Puerto del Rosario, the white sandy *playa* is usually sheltered and deserted. At the southern end is the large building of the Parador Nacional de Fuerteventura.
Pozo Negro Seventeen kilometres south east of Antigua is Pozo Negro, a small undeveloped beach, suitable for a picnic.

Accommodation

Accommodation in Fuerteventura is limited mostly to the three main tourist resorts. In the north around Corralejo, on the east coast at Castillo de Fuste and in the south at Costa Calma and Jandía. In Puerto del Rosario the best accommodation is at the Parador Nacional. Because of the lack of visitors in the past, there is practically no accommodation in the small villages. The Tourist Office in Puerto del Rosario will supply a list of hotels but does not book rooms. You do that at a travel agent *(viaje).* Although there is development in the south of Fuerteventura, most of the hotels and apartments can be booked only through package tour operators, most of which are in Germany. The majority of British visitors stay in Corralejo and Castillo de Fuste.

Corralejo

★★★★★Hotel — Tres Islas Carretera Playas de Corralejo. Tel: 86 60 00. 365 beds, including suites. Airconditioned, luxury hotel on the beach. Recently refurbished to a very high standard. Most rooms have terrace overlooking sea. Large heated swimming pool set in tropical gardens, TV lounge, night club, tennis courts, sauna, massage, hairdressing, children's playground, hobby club and entertainments. This is an elegant hotel with immediate access to the sand dunes and beach. Staff speak English.

★★★**Hotel — Oliva Beach** Carretera Playas de Corralejo. Tel: 86 61 00. 410 beds. Family hotel with a cheerful and informal atmosphere. Rooms overlook the beach. Large swimming pool with sunbed area. TV lounge, disco, entertainments programme, games room and playground.

★**Hotel Residencia — Corralejo** Calle Colon 12. Tel: 86 62 28. 19 beds. In town centre by sea. Modest, clean, inexpensive, Canarian. Plenty of restaurants and shops nearby.

★★**Bungalows — Los Barqueros** Carretera Puerto del Rosario. Tel: 86 60 72. 80 bungalows. Bar, restaurant, pool and garden. On edge of town and near to the beaches.

★★**Apartments — Corralejo Beach** In centre of town these apartments are clean, friendly and safe for young families. An adjoining restaurant serves good food. No lounge, TV or games room.

★★**Apartments — Hoplaco** Generalisimo Franco 40. Tel: 86 60 40. 104 apartments with plenty of amenities, swimming pool, restaurant, supermarket and parking.

★★**Apartments — Oliva Beach** Carretera Playas de Corralejo. Tel: 86 61 00. 44 apartments. Close to the Oliva Beach Hotel and the beach, nearby supermarket and travel agent.

Puerto del Rosario

★★**Hotel — Valeron** Calle Candelaria del Castillo. Tel: 85 06 16. 32 beds, with telephone. Breakfast only. Quiet hotel, close to port.

★★**Pension — Tamasite** León y Castillo. Tel: 85 02 80. 34 beds with telephone. No other facilities. In the main street and centre of town.

★★**Apartments — Ruben Tinguaro** Calle Juan XXIII 51. Tel: 85 10 88. 12 apartments with telephone. In town towards the north.

★★**Parador Nacional de Fuerteventura** Playa Blanca, Puerto del Rosario. Tel: 85 11 50. 46 beds. A low lying building by the sandy beach and overlooking the harbour and town of Puerto del Rosario. Elegantly furnished in Spanish style, the services include restaurant, bar, swimming pool, garden and parking.

Caleta de Fuste

★**Urbanisation - El Castillo** Caleta de Fuste. Tel: 87 80 46. 390 bungalows and apartments. Comfortably furnished, with terrace or garden patio in garden setting. Part of modern tourist holiday village, with public swimming pool, central plaza, yacht marina, shops, restaurants, entertainments, sandy beach, tennis, squash, windsurfing and diving. Good for families. 7kms from airport.

Tarajalejo

★★★**Hotel — Tofio** Carreterra de Tarajalejo. Tel: 87 00 50. 120 beds. Modern hotel in quiet position, close to beach in the south, 32 kms from the airport. Ten minutes walk to village shops and restaurant.

★**Apartments — Tarasa** Playa de Tarajalejo. Tel: 87 09 79. 47 fully furnished apartments close to the beach, near Tofio Hotel. Rather isolated, peaceful position in south. Village nearby.

Costa Calma

★★★★**Hotel — Casa Atlantica** Matorral, Jandía. Tel: 87 60 17. 145 beds. A well established hotel, just across the road from the marvellous Jandía beach. Plenty of facilities nearby, shops, bars and restaurants.

★★★**Hotel — Los Gorriones** Playa de la Barca. Tel: 87 08 50. 309 beds in well established family hotel, at the beginning of wonderful Jandía beach. Self contained with shops, sports facilities and entertainment. A la carte restaurant, parking. Windsurfing school on beach.

★★★**Hotel — Taro Beach** Canada de Río. Tel: 87 06 76. 140 beds in modern hotel. Isolated tourist resort. German oriented. Close to miles of sandy beach.

★★★**Hotel Apartments — Taro Beach** Canada de Río. Tel: 87 03 32. 262 apartments in newly built self contained urbanisation in the south. Fifteen minute walk to miles of beach.

Getting about

Roads

The main roads in Fuerteventura vary from very good to moderate. There is a big programme to improve many of the roads, including those to the smaller and most isolated villages. Traffic is mainly light and it moves very fast, except where there is a new development, when the movement of lorries can cause short delays. There are no car parking problems at present, except perhaps in the centre of Morro Jable. If you wish to drive away from the beaten track, then it is essential to use a jeep or a four-wheel drive vehicle, especially when you visit Cofete on the extreme south west coast.

It is well to remember that this is a large island when it comes to travelleing, and there are not a lot of petrol stations, especially in the Jandía peninsula. All but one close on Sunday, so fill up on Saturday. Recently opened is a 24-hour filling station, just south of Antigua on the GC610. You can have your car washed here, too.

Buses

The public bus service, Autobuses Transporte Fuerteventura, runs to all the main places on the island, but the service is run mainly for farmers and their families — although it will stop for anyone at the roadside, if hailed. Do not be surprised if a goat goes along, too! Very few tourists use this method of transport. There is no service on a Sunday or public holidays. The bus station in Puerto del Rosario is on Calle Alfonso XIII 25. Tel: 85 09 51.

Extract from bus time table

Puerto del Rosario to Corralejo and El Cotillo

Pto del Rosario	Tindaya	La Oliva	Corralejo	El Cotillo
		daily		
12.30	13.00	13.05	13.25	13.50
		Mondays to Fridays		
18.15	18.45	18.50	19.10	—
El Cotillo	**Corralejo**	**La Oliva**	**Tindaya**	**Pto Rosario**
		Mondays to Fridays		
—	07.30	07.50	07.55	08.25
		Saturdays, Sundays and holidays		
—	07.45	08.05	08.10	08.40

El Cotillo—Corralejo

El Cotillo	Corralejo		Corralejo	El Cotillo
		daily, except Saturdays		
07.30	08.10		13.30	14.10

Puerto del Rosario to Gran Tarajal

	Pto Rosario	Antigua	GranTarajal
daily	12.30	13.05	13.35
Mondays to Fridays	17.30	18.00	18.35
	GranTarajal	**Antigua**	**Pto Rosario**
daily	07.30	08.00	08.35
Mondays to Fridays	16.30	17.00	17.35

Puerto del Rosario to Morro Jable

Pto del Rosario	Gran Tarajal	Tara-jalejo	Costa Calma	Morro Jable
Tuesdays to Fridays only				
14.00	15.05	15.30	15.45	16.30
Morro Jable	**Costa Calma**	**Tara-jajelo**	**Gran Tarajal**	**Pro del Rosario**
Tuesdays to Fridays only				
06.00	06.45	07.00	07.25	08.30

Note: It is advisable to confirm times in advance.

Taxis

The main taxi rank in Puerto del Rosario is close to the port entrance and opposite the Bar Tinguaro. In Fuerteventura all the taxis are coloured cream and green and will carry four passengers Fares are expensive because of long distance travel. Agree on a price before you start your journey and when possible share a taxi. Examples of fares: Airport to Hotel Los Gorriones (78km) — 5400 pesetas (£27.83); Airport to Puerto del Rosario — 500 pesetas (£2.57)

To call a taxi in Puerto del Rosario: Tel: 85 00 59 or 85 02 16; in Corralejo: 86 61 08; in Morro Jable: 87 62 57; and in Gran Tarajal: 87 80 06.

Car hire

In Puerto del Rosario, Corralejo, Gran Tarajal, Costa Calma, Jandía and at hotels you will be able to rent a self-drive car. A deposit of 5000 pesetas (£26) is usually required. Vehicle insurance costs about 900 pesetas (£4.63) a day according to class of vehicle. Passenger personal insurance is optional but advisable at about 300 pesetas (£1.54) a day and includes all occupants. In most cases you need to be over 21 and to have held a licence for two years. Car Hire firms in Fuerteventura include:

Avis Corralejo. Tel: 85 02 61
Auto Soto Airport. Tel: 87 64 19
Autos Dominguez Airport. Tel: 85 12 50
Juan de Bethancourt Puerto del Rosario. Tel: 85 11 57.

(Opposite) *The wonderful white sands of the deserted beach along the coast of Jandia has still to be 'discovered'.* **(Overleaf)** *The hotel Tres Islas is built on the sand dunes in the north of Fuerteventura: the epitome of luxury in an almost isolated setting.*

Costs of hire depend on the size of the vehicle and the period of hire. For example:

- Seat Panda
  2000 pesetas (£10.30) per day; 12,000 pesetas (£61.85 per week
- Ford Escort
  3000 pesetas (£15.46) per day; 18,000 pesetas (£92.78) per week
- Jeep Suzuki
  4000 pesetas (£20.61) per day; 24,000 pesetas (£123.71) per week

Sometimes there is a charge for kilometres in excess of a basic number.

Petrol stations are generally closed on Sunday and public holidays. There is one at Antigua that is open twenty-four hours.

Excursions

Coach excursions and tours on Fuerteventura are organised by travel agents, who will take bookings at their offices. But mainly the tours are arranged by tour operator representatives in hotels and apartments. As tourism is still in its infancy here, there is not a wide choice of excursions.

Tour of the island

This is an all day tour and requires an early morning departure from either Corralejo in the north, or Jandia in the south; returning in the evening about 1900 hrs. Lunch will be included and stops will be made at Betancuria, the old capital with its fine cathedral; Lajares to see the lace-making; La Oliva for pictures of the Colonels' House (it is restored but not yet open for visitors); and to one of Fuerteventura's beaches for a swim. The tour will include a spectacular mountain drive. Tour cost 4000 pesetas (£20.61).

Jeep safari

This is a good trip for the young and adventurous who wish to see, off the beaten track beaches, and do not mind being driven on bumpy roads. Lunch is included. Price 4000 pesetas (£20.61).

Island of Los Lobos

Departures are from Corralejo, for a sea crossing to the tiny island of Los Lobos, which is a Nature Reserve. The excursion includes aquatic sports, swimming and walking on lovely beaches. Lunch is at Casa del Farero. Sometimes the trip is cancelled due to the rough seas between the islands.

Island of Lanzarote

An early morning departure by boat from Corralejo to Playa Blanca in the south of Lanzarote, where the tour continues by coach. This all day excursion will take you to visit the Fire Mountain and will drive to the north to see the Jameos de Agua caves and other sights. Price, including lunch, 8700 pesetas (£48.84).

Shark fishing

Departures from hotels in Jandía at 1030 hrs and return at about 1600 hrs. A pleasant day at sea, sailing along the coast with maybe the sight of a shark. Lunch included. Cost 5000 pesetas (£25.77). There is also 'My Lilli', a fishing trip from Morro Jable, 3500 pesetas (£18).

Jetfoil to Gran Canaria

The jetfoil leaves from the port at Morro Jable for a day excursion to Las Palmas, Gran Canaria for shopping or a coach tour of the north of the island, returning about 1700 hrs. Price 8440 pesetas (£43.50).

TWELVE

Fuerteventura's restaurants, nightlife and leisure activities

Restaurants

Because of the large distances between towns, eating out in restaurants tends to be very localised. Small Canarian bars often have a dining area, where the atmosphere is relaxed. Usually there is TV or radio, and if there is a football match being shown expect plenty of noisy cheering!

Prices for meals are similar to the rest of the Canaries, with the *menu del días* being about 800 pesetas (£4.12). In Corralejo and Caleta de Fuste the menus tend to be for the British taste with real 'English breakfasts' and 'Sunday roast dinner' being advertised. Down in the south around Morro Jable you see menus catering for the German and Scandinavian tourists.

No wine or beer is produced in Fuerteventura.

Here is a list of restaurants where we have eaten or which have been recommended to us.

Antigua

Molino Antigua Calle de Antigua a Puerto del Rosario. Old farmhouse by an interesting restored mill. Canarian dishes including *papas arrugas* and hot *mojo* sauce.

Betancuria

Bar Valtaraja In the old capital. Inexpensive menu.

Caleta de Fuste

Cervesria In Plaza. Chicken and chips, good for families, and cheap.

El Mirador Castillo Beach. Barbecue, live music except Wednesday.

La Frasquita Far side of bay, looks like a chapel. Excellent fish; order lobster day before.

La Perlita Near heated swimming pool. Good for steaks.

Pizzeria Upstairs in plaza. Good family restaurant.

Corralejo

Casa Juan Calle General Linares 5. Tel: 86 62 19. Good for fish. A bit pricey.

Chalo y Manuela Calle Isaac Peral 38. Swiss owned, pleasant decor.

Corralejo Beach In apartments. Canarian, good value.

El Patio Calle Betalla de Lepanto. Spanish, good value.

Fagin's In the plaza. Good steak, live music.

Oasis Tres Islas Hotel. Tel: 86 60 00. For a special night out. The restaurant of this luxury hotel has an imaginative menu, which is served with dexterity by a courteous staff.

Oscar Calle La Iglesia 9. Mexican and international.

El Cotillo

El Tostón In centre of village. Canarian, good for fish.

Lajita

Cuesta de la Pared. German run, good food with splendid view over beach.

Morro Jable

Casa Emillo Avenida del Mar. Good for meat dishes.

El Laja Avenida del Mar. International menu and fish.

Toni Pinte Avenida del Mar. International and fish.

Pozo Negro

Los Caracoles Unpretentious village restaurant near the sea. Sea food and *paella,* but rather high prices.

Puerto del Rosario

El Granero Calle Alcalde Alonso Patallo 8. Tel: 85 14 53. Open 1100 to 1500 and 1900 to midnight, closed Sunday. In centre of town, attractive. Canarian menu.

Tarajalejo

El Brasero Apartado de Correos 169, Gran Tarajal. In the countryside off the main road towards Tarajalejo. Attractive patio. Meat only, cooked on an open fire, generous portions, caters for coach parties. Live music and singing, camel and horse riding.

Gregorio Calle Cabrera Martin. Tel: 45 23 27. Well established, small, typical Canarian restaurant in village. Good for fish.

Nightlife

This is not an island to have a rave up at night. Entertainments are very local and mainly provided in the tourist hotels and local bars.

A cinema, the Marga, in **Puerto del Rosario,** shows films in Spanish.

There are discos in the following places.

Corralejo Freddy's, Calle La Iglesia; Las Camelias, Calle Crucero Canarias 13.

Gran Tarajal Pub Disco Roma, Playa Gran Tarajal.

Morro Jable Fama, Calle Nuestra Sra. del Carmen.

Puerto del Rosario Star, Calle Virgen de la Peña 15; Taifa, Calle Professor Juan Tadeo Cabrera.

Tarajalejo La Tabema, Apartments Taraxa

Caleta de Fuste Disco SOS (open from 2100 to 0300 hrs).

Shopping

Supermarkets are to be found in all the towns, villages and where there are apartments. Many of these sell fresh and frozen meats, fruit and vegetables, also household items. In Puerto del Rosario look for the La Pluma Rosa Supermarket. The goods are price tagged. Generally prices are a little higher in Fuerteventura than in the UK, although drinks and cigarettes are cheaper. Should you wish to buy goat's meat *(cabra)* most butchers *(carnicera)* will have a fresh supply. Roast kid, *(cabrito)* is delicious and tender like lamb. Some fresh fish is available but never cheap; try the Gran Tarajal market. Local goat's cheese *(queso blanco)* is very tasty; you can buy it in the Puerto del Rosario market.

Buying clothes locally

In the past when Fuerteventura had few tourists there was little requirement for boutiques and smart dress shops. However, with the advent of tourism, some places are now to be found in the resorts. The bigger hotels sell clothes with *couture* labels, and shoes and handbags to match. Beachwear, T-shirts and shorts hang outside in the streets of Corralejo and down at Morro Jable. But there are no superstores in Puerto del Rosario, or elsewhere, and generally it is better not to rely on getting a special outfit on the island. But you will find a good selection of windsurf and sports gear in some shops in Corralejo.

Souvenirs

Local hand-made embroidery can be purchased at Lajares, where you will see it being made, and at El Molina in Antigua. There is an *artesania* shop near the market in Puerto del Rosario and in some hotels. Hand made souvenirs are basketwork, pottery and

At Lajares a School of Embroidery is open to the public. Young girls with nimble fingers make delicate embroidery unique to the Canary Islands.

costume dolls. Other items in the tourist shops are likely to have been imported and labelled 'Fuerteventura'.

Sports

Because Fuerteventura has large beaches and mild weather, outdoor sports are very much part of a holiday for the energetic tourist.

Cycling

The main roads in Fuerteventura are quite suitable for cycling. They are mostly flat, except around Betancuria and parts of the west coast. Because of the size of the island, getting from north to south (160 km) involves a lot of leg muscle. Remember, too, that Fuerteventura can be very sunny and windy, but the peace and quiet of the countryside with its views makes pleasant cycling. Mountain bikes can be hired in Corralejo from **Tradewinds** for 600 pesetas (£3.09) per day.

Diving

The island has exceptionally clear waters for skin diving. The aquatic life is particularly good with a colourful variety of marine fauna. Amongst its most exotic are the parrot fish, little *cabrillas,* the huge sting ray, and the silvery barracuda. Facilities for scuba diving can be arranged by the **Marina of El Castillo de Fuste,** open from 1000 hrs. Six lessons for beginners cost 20,000 pesetas (£103); one dive using own equipment costs 2400 pesetas (£12.37) and the licence to dive 2000 pesetas (£10.30). **Diving School Feliz** operates at Morro Jable. Underwater Parks are being created at Corralejo and Jandia to help preserve the aquatic environment. At the same time it is hoped these will create tourist attractions under the sea. Underwater sports clubs are **Barakuda Club Diving Centre,** Corralejo. Tel: 86 62 43; **Robinson Club,** Jandía. Tel: 87 63 75.

Fishing

The waters around Fuerteventura have great wealth of fish and it is said there are 1,500 different species. Because of the warm waters that lie close to the island it is a perfect breeding ground. Good fishing all the year round can be had by fishing from the shore, by boat or underwater. Amongst the fish sought after are shark, swordfish, tunny, dorada, corva, sea bass, sea dace and eels. You will see the local fishermen amongst the rocks searching for octopus. There is a **Deep Sea Fishing School** in Corralejo. Tel: 85 13 29.

Football

Like in all the Canary islands, Fuerteventura has a football pitch in every town and village, and the game is played with enthusiasm from an early age. Inter-island matches create much excitement and support. The main football stadium is on the outskirts of Puerto del Rosario, south of the main road to the airport.

Sailing

Yacht marina facilities are available at Corralejo, Castillo de Fuste and soon at the new harbour of Morro Jable. A few boats also anchor off shore at Puerto del Rosario. El Castillo de Fuste is twelve kilometres from Puerto del Rosario. Nautical position 22° 23′ 25″ N. Latitude 13° 51′ 15″ W. The harbour has 150 berths with drinking water, 220 volt electrical connections, travel lift crane, fuel station, ship repair shop, weather service and permanent radio contact, UHF channel 16, MC channel 9. Vessels can be laid up in the boathouse. Beacons give off single green flashes with nautical range of six miles.

Tennis and squash

These sports can be enjoyed at most of the big hotels and some of the apartments. Racquets can be hired with a deposit of 2000 pesetas (£10.30); cost of play from 400 pesetas (£2.60) per hour.

Walking

Many people say that Fuerteventura has the best climate and best beaches in the archipelago. We would agree that it is a marvellous place for walking on beaches, both in the north but especially in the south, where there is plenty of scope for the keen walker. A pleasant walk can be had from Morro Jable, along the beach to the Los Gorriones Hotel (for refreshments) a distance of about 21 kms. Walks inland can prove worthwhile. Noel Rochford in his *Landscapes of Lanzarote and Fuerteventura* (see bibliography) gives some excellent advice and routes for enjoying walking. Do remember when walking that this is a large, dry island with a sparse population and the sun is very hot.

Windsurfing

Fuerteventura is only just being discovered as the perfect place for a windsurfing holiday; the winds on the coast provide excellent conditions for the sport. In July competitions are held along the Sotavento coast. Windsurfing schools can be found in Jandía, Corralejo and at Caleta de Fuste on the east coast. A beginners course of ten hours costs 17,000 pesetas (£87.62), a non-beginners ten-hours course costs 12,600 pesetas (£64.94). One hour windsurfing, including use of board, shoes and wet suit costs 1400 pesetas (£7.21). A number of windsurfing enthusiasts travel with motorcaravans, going to different parts of the island to find the best wind.

The Parador Nacional de Fuerteventura has a quiet position a few kilometres south of Puerto Rosario, overlooking the sea by a sandy beach.

THIRTEEN

Puerto del Rosario

The capital city

Puerto del Rosario, the capital of Fuerteventura, used to be called Puerto de las Cabras (Port of Goats), but in 1957 it was decided to improve its image by giving it a more attractive sounding name! Up to the end of the last century the island was divided into three municipalities, La Oliva, La Antigua and Betancuria, the last being the original capital of Fuerteventura.

The city is situated in a natural bay and incorporates a small port. The atmosphere is that of a town that has settled by the sea. Seen from afar the skyline has little to commend it to the traveller, seeming to have become a little lost with its town planning. A new promenade is being constructed which will greatly improve the seafront area.

In the harbour fishing boats and small cargo ships jostle for space along the quays. The arrival of the Trasmediterranea ferry is a time of much activity. A few yachts make use of the calm waters of the bay. At the northern end of the town a large electricity power station stands on the edge of the coast. The garrison buildings, which are a prominent feature of Puerto del Rosario, are important headquarters of the Spanish Foreign Legion. Impressive statues of foreign legionnaires are set in small gardens just off the Calle Almirante Lallemand. Nowadays only a small force of legionnaires is based in the capital.

Puerto del Rosario may seem to have little to offer the tourist, but for the ardent traveller it is a typical example of a quiet Canarian town. Going about their daily lives, the local people are always polite and helpful; often if there is a language problem — for very few speak English — they will go out of their way to show you your required destination, or find someone who is able to communicate with you.

For exploring the island, Puerto del Rosario makes a central base, with tourist areas and hotel accommodation being nearly equally divided between the extreme north and south.

City tour

There is not a great deal to see in Puerto del Rosario. It will take about an hour and a half to complete this walk-about.

The main street from the port is León y Castillo, which goes straight uphill northwards. On the left side you see the buildings of the **Town Hall** and **Police Station** (Tel: 85 07 50).

At the first main crossroads with Avenida 1 de Mayo stands the tall white **Iglesia de la Virgen del Rosario,** the island's premier church. This is the only building of distinction in the town, apart from the barracks of the Spanish Foreign Legion. Set in a rather austere plaza, the Church of the Virgin of Rosario is equally sparse inside. White walls and high wooden ceiling lead to a simple altar piece where the sacred image of the Virgin is venerated. Sitting quietly in this tranquil and lofty church, one is reminded of the past history of this poor island so often ransacked and ravaged by pirates. The principal fiesta in Fuerteventura is to the Virgen del Rosario, held from 1st to 7th October every year.

To reach the **post office** you turn left along the Avenida 1 de Mayo and it is number 58, on the left. If you wish to collect your mail you will need to turn the corner to a separate entrance, and go downstairs to a counter and ask for Lista de Correos. Take your passport for identification. Mail takes about ten days from the UK. The post office opens Monday to Friday 0900 to 1400 hrs, Saturday 0900 to 1300 hrs.

Further along the Avenida 1 de Mayo, on the opposite side to the post office, you come to number 33, the **Patronato de Turismo** (tourist office). It is on the first floor of the building of the Ministerio de Trabajo (Ministry of Public Works). Tel: 85 10 24. Open from 0830 to 1500 hrs, Monday to Friday.

A **market** is situated in the Plaza España. It is small and clean with limited supplies of meat, fruit and vegetables. Fresh and tasty white goat's cheese can be bought whole or in a piece by weight. A turning off Avenida 1 de Mayo, called Calle Fuerteventura, has a good butcher *(carniceria)* and next door a shop sells cooked chickens *(pollo asado)* and delicatessen foods.

Just up the road from the market is Artespaña, the Spanish government **handicraft shop,** selling a small selection of costume dolls, children's toys, embroidered cloths, ceramics, pottery and basket-work, most of which is made in Fuerteventura. Prices compare favourably with the souvenir shops in the hotel resorts. In the *artesania* shop you will probably find a young pretty shop assistant who will be delighted to practise her English, if you speak slowly. English is now being taught in the schools to higher grade students, but because of the scarcity of English-speaking tourists, it is difficult for the language to be practised.

The **Trasmediterranea ferry office** is at number 46, León y Castillo. Tel: 85 08 77. It is here that you can make reservations on the inter-island car ferry and the ferry to Cadiz. Open 0900 to 1300 and 1630 to 1900 hrs, Monday to Saturday. The **Medical Centre and Hospital** is on the southern edge of town, on the inland side of the main road to the airport (al Aeropuerto). There is a petrol station along the Calle Secundino and opposite is the useful supermarket, **La Pluma Roja** — you will see the red feather sign by the entrance. Should you need a chemist, go to Calle San Roque 15 (quite close to the Tourist Office); the *farmacia,* open from 0900 to 1300 and 1600 to 1900 hrs, is next to the Banco de Bilbao.

Shopping in Puerto del Rosario is done at a leisurely pace, no one hurries, often conversation is more important than the purchase and you will be kept waiting. So allow time for your visit to Puerto del Rosario. The Tourist Office have a delightful sticker that says, *Stress, que va! Yo descanso en Fuerteventura.* (If you suffer from stress then relax in Fuerteventura!)

Do not expect too much of your tour of Puerto del Rosario. There are no museums or big stores and the small shops are scattered. Yet it is the very lack of grandeur that is the delight of Fuerteventura, a simplicity that is rare in this busy world of today.

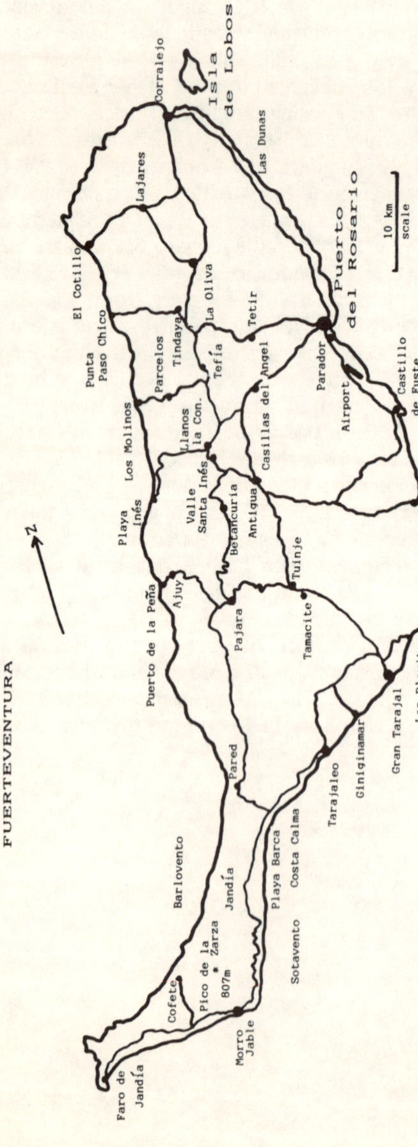
FUERTEVENTURA
N
Isla de Lobos
Corralejo
Las Dunas
Lajares
El Cotillo
La Oliva
Tetir
Puerto del Rosario
10 km scale
Punta Paso Chico
Parcelos
Tindaya
Tefía
Casillas del Angel
Parador
Airport
Castillo de Fuste
Los Molinos
Llanos la Con.
Playa Inés
Valle Santa Inés
Betancuria
Antigua
Pozo Negro
Tuinje
Ajuy
Puerto de la Peña
Pajara
Tamacite
Las Playitas
Gran Tarajal
Giniginamar
Tarajaleo
Pared
Barlovento
Jandía
Playa Barca
Costa Calma
Pico de la * Zarza 807m
Sotavento
Cofete
Morro Jable
Faro de Jandía

FOURTEEN

Touring Fuerteventura

Island tour 1

Puerto del Rosario — Las Dunas — Corralejo — Isla de Los Lobos (about 30 km; a ½ day excluding crossing to Los Lobos)

Taking the route northwards along the coast, the land is flat and sparse of vegetation. On the outskirts of Puerto del Rosario are the large electricity power station and the important desalination plant. Fish canning factories packing sardines and tuna fish add considerably to the island economy. These are exported to the European market, and the quality of the fish canned makes it worth while seeking it out in the supermarkets.

A good road makes it a pleasant drive with sea views the entire way to Corralejo, thirty eight kilometres north of Puerto del Rosario. Several small dirt-track roads lead down to little undeveloped bays and coves. The coast is earmarked for tourist development, however, and already several foreign entrepreneurs have started small *urbanizacións* of villas. Many are unoccupied for much of the time and have a rather forlorn appearance. One of the new developments being built on the sea side of the road, near **Puerto Oliva,** is a sanatorium for people coming from Europe to recuperate in the sunshine and clear air of Fuerteventura.

Within fifteen kilometres of Corralejo, the landscape changes completely, for this is the area known as **Las Dunas** where sometimes the edges of the road can be obliterated by sand. Seen for the first time the great sand dunes on either side of the road can be quite stunning. This is the nearest thing to one's idea of a desert. It is a natural place of unique beauty, now designated as the **Parque Natural de las Dunas de Corralejo y la Isla de Los Lobos.** The site is an eco-system of great scientific value: the flora being resistant to strong winds and able to survive with little water and few nutrients.

Regarding fauna, the main species is the lizard of Haria, endemic to Fuerteventura and Lanzarote, which though small has a large appetite and manages to eat quantities of the insects common to the Canary Islands. Bird life is plentiful close to the sea, in the sand dunes, and this is a favourite resting place for migrating birds who seem to pass by night. Isla de Los Lobos is close by off the northern shore.

The beaches are entirely natural, with small rocky pools and clean water and are a marked contrast to the wild landscape of the interior. The light is brilliant for the sands are very fine, almost white, the sea a turquoise green, whilst above the blue sky rarely has a cloud. Just one warning: on rare occasions, when the *sirocco* blows and the skies are full of sand it is preferable to stay indoors with a good book!

Near the extreme north of the island just four kilometres before Corralejo, two large hotels have been erected, looking rather out of place amongst the flatness of the area. Hotel Oliva Playa, three-star, and Hotel Tres Islas, five-star, both belong to the excellent hotel chain, Iberotel, which has vast experience of giving value for money in hotels in mainland Spain and the Balearic Islands as well as the Canary Islands. Three islands — Fuerteventura, Los Lobos and Lanzarote — can indeed be seen from the Hotel Tres Islas which is set right on the sand dunes at the edge of the blue Atlantic, with all that is expected of a first class hotel. At present visitors are mostly from Germany and Scandinavia, so most of the entertainments and menus are geared for their pleasure. Nevertheless, when you make it known that you are British, an attentive staff including English-speaking members will endeavour to make you feel welcome. There is plenty of sport and entertainment during the day for young and more mature holidaymakers, offering alternatives to the beach or hotel pools: video shows and dancing nightly in the hotel or disco, quiz games, folk dancing and cabaret shows provide some of the attractions.

Close to the hotels are some apartments, two supermarkets and a boutique. Both apartment blocks have travel agents, Viajes Insular and Viajes Ultramar Express, where the staff have a reasonable knowledge of English and are helpful.

Driving around the north eastern tip of Fuerteventura, the bright white sand dunes continue while the Atlantic rollers increase as they surge through the channel called El Rio, which divides Fuerteventura and **Isla de Los Lobos.**

This is the place much favoured by naturists who use discreet areas in the sand dunes for total sun bathing. Wind surfing is much in evidence in all the Canary Islands, especially so in Fuerteventura off the *playas* of Corralejo (and down south off the Jandia peninsula). Several good fish restaurants are to be found along the beaches where you can sit on the patio looking out over the translucent waters towards Lobos and the volcanic peaks of Lanzarote, while your fresh fish is being barbecued. Restaurant la Galera has an international menu and is open late in the evening. Close by, the Corintia Restaurant is owned by Don Demetrio who will ensure that you have an enjoyable meal.

The area around Corralejo is being developed into a major tourist resort, with projected hotels and apartments going up in all directions. Sailing, underwater swimming and windsurfing provide plenty of outdoor sport. Along the shores the sandy beaches and rocky inlets are of much interest to crab hunters and shell collectors.

Corralejo, once a small lively fishing village, has gained in importance with the extension of the harbour; now it is used not only by fishing boats which go as far as the Sahara coast, but by the ferries to Lanzarote and excursion boats to Lobos. An increasing number of yachts and pleasure boats are using its modern facilities.

The small town has several supermarkets, tourist shops and all the usual utilities, including travel agents, taxi and car hire, petrol station, garage and banks. There is a selection of restaurants and bars, Freddies Disco being very popular at night. Coach tours that stop in Corralejo always recommend tourists to enjoy the splendid ice cream dishes and cheesecakes that are especially prepared for holidaymakers.

Corralejo is very popular with British holidaymakers; a number of bars, restaurants and boutiques are British owned and English newspapers are sold in the shops. Because of the good conditions for windsurfing there is quite a young element in the town, but thankfully they are not badly-behaved and indeed their rainbow coloured sails add much to the charm of the seashore.

Isla de Los Lobos takes its name from the seals (*lobos marinos*) which once haunted the local waters. It is said that Godifer de la Salle, a Norman knight, was marooned here during an expedition to Lanzarote and that he survived only by killing and eating seals.

From Corralejo the tiny island is only three kilometres off shore. It lies in the waters known as the Bocaina, derived from the Spanish word *boca* (mouth) because the waters are so full of fish that they surge along like a 'mouthful'. The fishing in the area is said to be the best in the Canaries and can be done from a boat or with snorkel and harpoon.

The island, which is 6.5 sq kms, is used by fishermen but no one

Corralejo Beach Apartments, in the centre of town, are clean and suitable for families with children, who will love the good-sized pool.

lives on Lobos. Excursions from Corralejo take tourists to the island for swimming and a beach barbecue.

While on this tiny island you can enjoy some good snorkelling or take a walk of about ten kilometres out to Faro de Lobos and also climb Montaña Lobos, a really wild and desert-like landscape with splendid views. Naturalists will be interested in the different types of flora that grow here, such as the ice plant, *mesembryanthemum crystallinum,* which years ago was used for extraction of soda. Los Lobos is now a Nature Reserve where no development is allowed. Remember that it can be windy and hot here and there is no shade, so a hat is essential, and so is comfortable footwear.

Island tour 2

Corralejo – Lajares – El Cotillo – La Oliva – Puertito de los Molinos – Tetir – Puerto del Rosario (about 87 kms; a ½-day drive without lingering at El Cotillo)

Nine kilometres south of Corralejo, on the GC600, a turning west goes to Lajares and Cotillo. This is a rather narrow road which goes through lava rock and *malpais* (wastelands) created by volcanic eruptions; yet one can see where in the past much effort has been made to try and cultivate the soil. Small fields are marked out with lava stone walls, even the odd fig tree is encircled to stop the goats from browsing its green leaves. Ruins of old stone houses, evidence of past habitation, look sad and lost. Every now and then a herd of goats will meander along the road, oblivious of travellers and one wonders what they will find to chew because, apart from the *aulaga* (thorn bush) there is little else to be seen. However all the goats seem to be in very good condition and grow to a huge size, looking very fiercesome with curved horns and long shaggy beards, and coats which are a thick mixture of brown, black and white hair. If your drive is in early spring you will see, in some of the low lying fields, banks of yellow flowers *(sonchus).* They make a colourful carpet against the brown, stony soil.

Lajares is a small cluster of farmers' houses, with a bar and supermarket. A new tourist attraction has been opened recently as it is a convenient stopping place for coach parties: a small **School of Embroidery** allows visitors to watch the nimble-fngered ladies sewing the intricate open drawn thread work that is typical of the Canaries. With deft hands they sit at a long wooden frame, the cloth drawn tightly across, as their fingers flick in and out with amazing speed — nevertheless a time-consuming task in these days of machinery. The tablecloths are expensive to buy but are a real joy to possess and with care can last a life-time. A small tourist shop next door offers an assortment of locally made articles. A bar and toilets make this a useful stopping place.

From Lajares it is seven kilometres to **El Cotillo,** a small fishing village on the north west coast of Fuerteventura. The village has some narrow one-way streets. A seventeenth-century watchtower, La Torre de Rico Roque is a feature. To the north of the village is a series of quiet sandy beaches and fishing can be had from the rocky points. This area has been earmarked for tourist developments, its lonely peaceful location having great appeal for those who appreciate solitude and remoteness.

This is a nice place to bring your children because in the small coves there are shallow pools which have clear warm water and clean sands. Should you wish to have a change from these beaches you can take a long walk along the coast to Faro de Tostón and beyond. In fact, if you feel really energetic and have time to spare you can continue on past Cortijo de la Costilla and through Casas de Majanicho (you may see windsurfers here), around the headland and into Corralejo, a 22km walk which takes about four hours.

Another alternative, when in El Cotillo, is to walk or drive down a dusty lane to the left, southwest of the village. Here is a wild, flat plateau of wasteland above shallow cliffs, below which is a usually deserted, long sandy beach. When the wind is strong you will witness the wonderful spectacle of foaming seas, with huge Atlantic rollers pounding their white spume against the sandy shore. Only a few sea birds will keep you company as they swoop and dive amongst the crashing waves.

Returning by car from El Cotillo to Lajares on the same road, it is possible to take a turning to La Oliva ten kilometres south. As one leaves Lajares behind, the road affords a splendid view of windmills depicting two different uses — the one on the left is for corn grinding, while the other is for pumping water from the subsoil.

La Oliva is a noble town which has played an important part in the history of the island. Many aborigine artefacts have been found within the municipality, including fertility idols which the ancient races worshipped. In the fifteenth century the Norman conquistadors, Jean de Bethencourt and Godifer de la Salle, used La Oliva as a base for further conquests. When, in 1703, the Canary Islands ceased to be ruled by the nobility and passed to a central government in Tenerife, the ruling military officer, the 'Colonel'

The Casa de los Coroneles (The Colonels' House) at La Oliva, inland towards the north end of Fuerteventura.

who was in charge in La Oliva, became a person of great importance, in fact the chief personage on the island.

The **Casa de los Coroneles** (Mansion of the Colonels) was for many years the centre of social and political life in Fuerteventura. This magnificent structure remains to testify to the importance of La Oliva in the past. When in the nineteenth century the port of Cabras (now Puerto del Rosario) grew in importance, the political and economic life of the island moved there. Now the Casa de los Coroneles, which belongs to the Bravo de Laguna family, is being restored. This old fortress palace has a facade that includes a coat of arms, crowned by a small cross. Carved wooden balconies line the front of the building, two turrets at each end give a picture of symmetrical balance. It is reputed that the original building contained 365 doors and windows; we shall have to see if they are still there when the restoration is completed!

The Casa del Capellan (Chaplain's House), a smaller palace, is also of note. It has a huge wooden door decorated with Aztec designs thought to have been influenced by seafaring merchants visiting Mexico and Latin America.

The only religious building in La Oliva is the parish church, Iglesia de Nuestra Señora de Candelaria. A sturdy fortress-like stone building, white washed, except for the tall bell tower, it stands in a prominent position, its buttressed exterior walls giving evidence of its past use as a sanctuary from marauding pirates. Inside, its enormous proportions contain three naves, which have paintings by Juan de Miranda. There are many carvings of the saints. The holy relic of the image of Nuestra Señora de Candelaria is kept high above the altar.

On the second of February each year, in La Oliva, a fiesta is held to honour the Virgen de la Candelaria (of Tenerife). This is a four-day celebration of religious fervour and joyful festivity. The first day the religious relic is paraded, held on a dais at shoulder level, by four men. With due solemnity it is taken round the church square, while prayers are said and hymns are sung.

In the afternoon and during the next two days there are many sports events, children's and folk dancing. It culminates on the last day with the events like Canary wrestling, and a fireworks display. The entire town enters into this festive occasion, all dressed in new clothes. Wine flows freely, bands play and it is a gay, animated scene set under cloudless skies. Everyone, including tourists, is welcome to join in the celebrations and the Carnival.

In La Oliva there is a post office and small shop situated at the northern end of the main street.

Around the town is a wide plain and various sisal plantations are seen, this being once the main agricultural product of Fuerteventura. Old windmills and grazing goats make up the sparse scenery. Towards the mountains rabbits, partridge, turtle doves, pigeons and exotic gangas, a species of African game bird exclusive to the island, give a little sport for the hunters.

Continuing the journey south from La Oliva on the GC600, a turning off westwards leads to **Tindaya,** a small town of pleasant simplicity in an extremely dry area. Behind the houses we see the volcanic peak of Montaña Tindaya, which the Guanches venerated as a sacred and holy mountain. It is said that here they killed young goats and offered them in sacrifice to their gods. Important relics have been discovered on the summit, and some cave drawings and engravings can be seen, but it is a stiff climb up the rocky mountain to look at them.

Returning to the GC600 and going towards Puerto del Rosario, you will notice Montaña Quemada (the burnt mountain) rising out of the flat plain, notable as the place where a monument has been erected to honour Miguel de Unamuno (1864-1936), the great Spanish thinker and writer, who was exiled to Fuerteventura because of his political views. His love of the island, its peace and beauty, led to many eloquent verses. 'A rock thirsting in the sun, Fuerteventura, a treasure of health and honesty, may God guard you for ever from super abundance.'

A secondary road leads off from the GC600 just south of the Unamuno monument which is a short route to Betancuria, the old capital, but on that road you will drive through really wild desert scenery. The Agricultural Colony near **Tefia** is making an effort to cultivate the plain but it is a difficult project.

Beyond Tefía you can turn right, signposted to **Puertito de los Molinos**, and make a short detour (14 km) down to the west coast. A newly made road passes by flat arid fields. A restored windmill makes an attractive picture against the distant brown and ochre landscape, here and there herds of goats munch their way on the stony ground. Passing through the small settlement of La Parcelas (once called Colonis García Escamez), where some agricultural progress is being made, the road then drops down quite steeply for two kilometres into a valley where, at the bottom, a few fishermen's houses lie close to the shore, at Puertito de los Molinos. If it has been raining the water flows down the *barranco* (gorge) and you will have to cross a ford to reach this hamlet. You may like to picnic here.

Back up the same way, returning to the GC600, we continue southwards to **Tetir,** formerly a separate municipality but today part of the island's capital. The town is in a wide valley where some of the main cereal crops are grown. In the distance, looking north, the mountain called the Devil's Claw can be seen, a title explained by the dark spiky shapes. From Tetir it is but nine kilometres to the capital Puerto del Rosario.

Island tour 3

Puerto del Rosario — Casillas del Angel — La Ampuyenta — La Antigua — Tuinje — Pájara — Ajuy — Puerto de la Peña — Betancuria — Valle Santa Inés — Llanos de la Concepción — Puerto del Rosario (about 103 km; full day drive)

A central tour of the island can be made from Puerto del Rosario, taking an inland highway, the GC610, westwards from the city in the direction of La Antigua. The first place of importance is **Casillas del Angel** with its unusual neo-colonial style church. It has a bell tower of black masonry. The little village is scattered around in a rather haphazard manner.

After a short distance the road divides with a detour going to

Betancuria. The main road goes on to **La Ampuyenta,** with its walled Church of San Pedro de Alcantara. On the outskirts of La Antigua is El Molino (the windmill), now a premier stopping point for all tourist excursions. This two-hundred-year-old windmill is now fully restored and makes a beautiful picture. Visitors are allowed inside to see the corn being ground, and a custodian will do his best to explain the workings. There is a large car park.

Set in attractive gardens full of cactus, flowers and shrubs, is a large restaurant and bar. A small gift shop sells a range of simple hand-made souvenirs; the lady in the shop is busy with her hand-drawn needlework when not serving customers. Meals are served quickly in the restaurant and prices are average. The toilets are clean. If you only want a snack, try the soup; it is almost a meal and very tasty. For a cool drink ask for *sangria,* which is always served in a jug for two or more. Consisting usually of red wine, brandy, sparkling mineral water, lots of cut up oranges and lemons, with ice cubes, it is a typical Spanish drink.

La Antigua is a large town with a definite African flavour: low white-washed houses have flat roofs and shuttered windows. Many of the side roads are unmade tracks; dogs, chickens and goats wander about but few people are seen. Tall palm trees and small plantations of alfalfa (used for animal feeding) make patches of brilliant green; a few vegetables are cultivated, water being drawn from the wells.

La Antigua is one of the oldest towns on the island, and for a short period from 1834 to 1835 it was the capital. In the centre plaza is a sturdy white church with a tall bell tower, surrounded by pretty gardens and avenues of palm trees. The 8th September is the fiesta, Our Lady of La Antigua. Today, La Antigua's latest acquisition are traffic lights and a 24-hour petrol station.

Going further south along the GC160, one has fine views of the low reddish-brown mountains, the bright light casting shadows in patterns of different hues. The open vistas and space on every side create a feeling of peace and relaxation. This is not a drive for anyone craving excitement, unless you enjoy dodging goats! Should you be in need of refreshment, make a stop at a small wayside restaurant which lies by itself at the side of the main road, a few kilometres north of **Agua de Bueyes.** Bar Gaira is typical of many Canarian bars: from the outside unobtrusive and quiet and inside all modern, gleaming and clean. Whether you have drinks and *tappas* (snacks) at the bar or order a meal at the table, the service will be polite and friendly. Should you wonder what to order, the *señor* will be delighted for you to step into the kitchen, where his wife and daughter will smile happily as your nose advises you which of the tasty stews to select. You could be surprised at the reasonable bill at the end of the meal.

Near Tiscaminita a new farming project is the Bio Farm Laestanca, where tomatoes and other vegetables are being grown organically. Towards the east lie the dreary Malpais Chico and Malpais Grande, where the lava wasteland and rocks are from the volcanoes Caldera de la Laguna, Caldera de Liria and Caldera de las Arrabales.

The Battle of Tamacite

In 1740 English and Berber corsairs attacked people living on the Montañeta de Tamacite and in the village of Tuinje, robbing and looting the houses. They also seized two families who were hiding in the Church of San Miguel. However, the country folk rallied and armed only with sticks, and using their camels as a barrier, they managed to frighten and beat off the invaders. The town of Tuinje celebrates this brave victory every 13th October, with the Fiesta de San Miguel.

A few miles on is **Tuinje,** site of the historic battle of Tamacite against the English pirates. (All seems forgiven these days!) Tuinje once had a large population, being a farming centre, but now its main crop is just tomatoes. You will probably stop in town for petrol.

Our central tour goes no further south but turns westwards to Pájara on the GC620, passing several ruined dwellings, for it is a place of past agricultural activity. When the road reaches **Toto,** situated in a narrow valley, the sudden sight of waving palm trees and small areas of cultivation is welcome after the harshness of the arid fields and lava stone walls. In the warm shelter of the valley, tomatoes and vegetables are grown, bright bougainvillea and poinsettia bloom outside the little square white washed houses.

Pájara (meaning little bird) is noted especially for its parish church. The main entrance (just off the main road) has Aztec style sculptures over its huge doors. The shapes of suns, serpents, pumas and plumed crowned heads are carved in stone. The mixture of Gothic and Aztec designs dating from the mid sixteenth century is a fascinating sight in such a remote place. The stone work is in good order and the blocks have a perfect fit. The main entrance is topped by a triangular pediment. Inside the church the high altar dates from the eighteenth century. There is also an interesting Baroque confessional box, its dark wood heavily carved. Behind the church, a large building is the Cultural Centre, it includes a library and restaurant. Down by the river is a spacious carpark — though there is no parking problem in the village — and Pajara boasts it has a swimming pool.

Pájara has an important role as the municipal administrative centre for the whole of the Jandía peninsula. Many of the hotels in the south have staff who live in the district of Pájara.

While in Pájara it is possible to make an excursion of about ten kilometres to visit **Ajuy** and **Puerto de la Peña.** This is a very pretty drive off the beaten track, and when you arrive you can picnic or go to the little fish restaurant by the harbour, for a real Canarian meal. You will be surprised on this good road to find yourself in a verdant *barranco* (gorge) full of tamarisk and palm trees and, sadly, some abandoned houses. By Mezquez a scattering of small homesteads have chickens and goats roaming about; it is an utterly peaceful scene with a little stream flowing down to the Barlavento coast. In summertime fishermen from the village put to sea and bring back vast quantities of fish which is then, because of its good quality, flown direct to Las Palmas. One venerable sailor asserts that from April to September more fish is caught off this coast than anywhere else in the Canaries; but in winter the seas are often too rough for fishing. Should you like walking you will enjoy the twenty minutes it takes from Puerto de la Peña, going right up a well worn path, past the black beach to the top of a low cliff, where you can look down into Caleta Negra. Here are some fantastic natural caverns, and further on, at Peña Horadada, there's a huge volcanic rock with a hole leading into the sea. Choose a fine day for this venture for the wind and seas along this western coast can be really wild. At the moment all is totally unspoilt here, but will the new road bring modernisation?

On your return to Pajara, take a turning to your left, signposted Betancuria, then you will start to view some of the finest mountain scenery in the island. The route is along a rather narrow road with a reasonably good surface and steep bends penetrating high into the mountain range. All round the rich red soil is bare but for cactus struggling to grow in the rock crevices. As greater heights are reached there are immense panoramas of old, extinct volcanic peaks, some in curious shapes, all bathed in a warm glow of sunlight.

The purity of the air and the stillness are part of the magic that is Fuerteventura. At a certain point on the road the coastline is seen, with the Atlantic stretching out endlessly presenting a contrasting colour. The highest point has a view of the **Canyon del Rio Palma**

The Aztec designs on the carved stone portal are an interesting feature of the church at Pajara, and are presumably the work of a sixteenth-century craftsman who had returned from the New World.

Betancuria, the old capital of the island, attracts many tourists, who always visit the ancient cathedral, Iglesia de Santa Maria, rebuilt in the early seventeenth century on a grand scale. It still has an air of its past magnificance.

and the **Canyon de la Peña.** In the valley is a sanctuary of the Virgin of Sorrows, patron saint of Fuerteventura. The fifteenth-century alabaster image of Our Lady is much revered; a pilgrimage is made every September and people travel from all over the island to worship at the shrine.

On reaching Vega de Rió de Palma, you have an optional detour to visit the reservoir Presa de la Penitas and the tiny Chapel, Nuestra Señora de la Peña. You will have to leave your car in the village and walk about five kilometres, so wear comfortable, low heeled shoes. The valley is very attractive with tall pine trees and plots of cultivated land; your route is along a good track but it is a bit of a scramble as you near the reservoir. The white chapel looks minute against the steep slope of the mountain. Be careful as you get near, the track becomes quite steep. Inside this chapel dedicated to the island's patron Saint all is quiet. You may wish to add your name to the visitors' book.

Back again in your car and on the GC620 you continue this lovely mountain drive. After reaching a height of about some six hundred metres the road starts to descend and some vegetation is seen with the occasional homestead. Here and there a lonely fig tree, with its stone wall encirclement, flourishes — even the odd almond tree will be in blossom if you travel that way in January.

The ancient capital of Fuerteventura, **Santa Maria de Betancuria,** lies 27 kms south west of Puerto del Rosario, and is still the second place of importance in the island. It was founded by the Norman conqueror, Jean de Bethencourt; he felt that it was safer to live in the centre of the island away from attacking pirates. Hidden away in the heart of the mountains, this historic old town has now been declared a national monument. All that remains of its past glory is a quiet little community of about five hundred inhabitants and a large number of goats, but there are some historical monuments which are well worth seeing.

Arriving at Betancuria by the road from Pájara, the **Museo Arqueologico** is on the right side of the main road. This is a real delight to visit, even those who do not usually like museums will enjoy walking round this tiny treasury of ancient historic relics. The first room is not unusual with its skulls and bones of bygone Guanches, and bowls, tools and weapons to give an idea of their way of life. In a further room a picture of Jean de Bethancourt helps to fill out the history of events, swords and goblets show the grandeur of the nobility. But it is outside in the stone paved courtyard that the spell of the past is felt, in the tiny stone-floored rooms where ancient cooking utensils, agricultural tools and furniture are all displayed in a delightfully casual array.

Upstairs (mind the rickety staircase) there is a tiny room with a four-poster bed, looking just as it must have looked when last used. A pot and a small pair of lady's dainty high-heeled shoes are under the bed. It is quite the most informal museum you will ever enjoy. Outside stand two bronze cannon.

A little further down the road on the same side as the museum is the Mayor's house. Opposite, there is a small bar with a cool patio and tables set for meals. It has a car park and toilet.

Continuing along the main street which winds over a dry river bed, the mighty edifice of the cathedral, **Iglesia de Santa Maria de Betancuria,** stands high above. In the fifteenth century Bethencourt built a church which was the first episcopal seat in the archipelago, but it was destroyed by fire in 1539 by Berber Corsairs and the cathedral we see today was built in the seventeenth century. Its architectural style shows a strong Moorish influence with small windows and graceful tower. But gracing the sidewall is a very fine example of a typical Canarian pine wood balcony, beautifully carved. In the cathedral patio the deep well still has water.

The cathedral building is perfecly white washed. It has an imposing and highly decorated carved wooden doorway. Inside, the high altar is seventeenth-century Baroque and three vaulted niches catch the eye, two saints at the side with the Virgin and Child in the centre. At the rear of the cathedral deeply ornamented chairs are set like thrones under a wooden canopy; these were used by the nobility in days gone by. To one side is the image of Saint Buenaventura set on a plaque; this is much venerated and is paraded at the fiesta on 14th July each year.

It is said that, because of past sieges, there are hideaway holes and escape doors set high in the roof. Underneath the huge flagstone floor are the tombs of past Betancurians. In the sacristy are kept many precious relics: the Conquest Banner, Archbishop's regalia, crosses and candlesticks. A further chapel is now under restoration, its walls have wonderful murals, depicting religious scenes.

A few yards from the cathedral is a souvenir shop, and the lady there is the custodian of the cathedral and has the keys. When coach parties arrive she gives a demonstration of how goats' cheese is made; this may be purchased in the shop.

Walk along the valley road a little further and you will see the ruins of a Franciscan Monastery in which lived the Saint Diego de Alcala, who preached the gospel in the Canary Islands, especially to the sick and poor, and was canonised in 1558. Now only a single Gothic window, a few columns and some outer walls remain. On the other side of the valley is the recently restored Ermita de San Diego de Alcala, a hermitage built over a cave where the Spanish monk prayed. Further restoration is being done by the Ministry of Culture to a former convent which lies on the hill at the back of the village. This will eventually house an important library and archives.

Driving northwards from Betancuria the road again gives very fine panoramic views over the mountain ranges. There is a feeling of being on top of the world as the road affords vistas across to the sea on both sides of the island at once, with the bare red rocks of the mountains and valley in between.

Passing through **Valle Santa Inés,** with its cluster of palm trees, you reach **Llanos de la Concepción.** From the Bar Garcia you can hike to the Embalse de los Molinos, which is the largest reservoir in Fuerteventura. This is reputed to be a good place for bird watching. Back on the main road across the flat plains, with a few windmills in disrepair and young girl goat minders wearing white sun bonnets, after three kilometres, we join the GC610 and continue on to Casillas del Angel, which we visited on the way out, and back to **Puerto del Rosario,** with its rather confusing crossroads, and finally reach the centre of town.

Island tour 4

Puerto del Rosario — Aeropuerto Estancas — Caleta de Fuste — Pozo Negro — La Antigua — Las Playitas — Gran Tarajal (about 97 km; a ½-day drive)

An alternative to taking the GC610 to the south of the island is to leave Puerto del Rosario on the coastal highway marked *Aeropuerto*. It is only a short distance to Playa Blanca with its small sandy beach. Close by is the **Parador Nacional.** Set by the sea it has good views towards Puerto del Rosario. The **Aeropuerto Estancas** is located at sea level. Charter aircraft arrive daily throughout the year from Europe. There is a daily service to Las Palmas, Tenerife and Lanzarote and a weekly flight direct to Seville and Madrid by Iberia Airways.

The airport building is spacious, sparsely filled with a couple of shops that sell newspapers, books, sweets, a few souvenirs and flowers, and an Information desk, luggage trollies, bar and clean toilets with facilities for the disabled. At present there is no charge for parking outside the airport, which is closed at night. There are

The yacht marina at Caleta de Fuste, a developing tourist resort on the east coast of Fuerteventura.

taxis available for arriving visitors — see Chapter 11 for further details.

The landscape around the airport is quite flat and arid. At Playa El Matorral the scrubland by the beach can be used for sunbathing and a picnic. Across the road, inland, are a number of roadside restaurants, used by the locals as well as the passing holidaymakers. Amongst these El Rancho and El Chaparral have Canarian menus that will include roast lamb and goat, although these days you are more likely to get chips rather than Canarian *papas arrugas*.

This dreary countryside continues until you reach the new tourist development of **El Castillo de Fuste** and Playa Caleta de Fuste.

The old *castillo* is an eighteenth century watch tower around which an *urbanización* has grown. With swimming pool and tennis courts, restaurants and shops the area seems self-contained. Two tier accommodation consists of a lounge, kitchen with eating bar, twin-bedded room and good bathroom facilities. Units are well equipped with crockery, cutlery and fridge.

Caleta de Fuste's small harbour has a good yacht marina with water and electric points and two hard slipways with launching bay. The gates are locked at night. The sandy beach is in between the two developments and wind surfing is available with equipment for hire and tuition for beginners. Remember that Fuerteventura can suffer strong winds.

The coast road then turns inland and goes across old *malpais* (volcanic wasteland) but, being a new road, the surface is good. As there is very little traffic, travel can be fast. Occasionally one sees a small dwelling where, apart from a couple of chickens and a dog, the only sign of life is the inevitable herd of goats. At a signposted junction a turning goes east to **Pozo Negro,** eleven kilometres away, at present devoid of any modern development. It is not possible to continue south on a tarmac road from Pozo Negro, you have to backtrack. The other branch at the junction goes north and heads for La Antigua where one can join the C610 southwards through Tuineje to Gran Tarajal.

It is on the road leading into Gran Tarajal that you see a factory where a thriving new industry has started, the making of *majorero,* a splendid cheese made from goat's milk. Fuerteventura's herds of goats are particularly hardy and give an excellent yield of milk. It is reported that about 40,000 are kept outside in open stables, and that another 20,000 are grazing wild. They are one of the distinctive features of the island.

Two kilometres before Gran Tarajal, at the beginning of a palm grove, a turning to the left takes you eastwards to **Las Playitas.** This is a delightful small fishing village in a sheltered bay. At the southern end a deserted greyish sandy beach is reached by going down a dirt track road; there swimming is possible when the sea is calm.

The main part of the village is clustered at the eastern end of the bay, which lies under a high cliff face. With only a shallow pebble rock beach, it is used mainly by the local fishermen who go out daily in their fragile one-man boats, some of which have engines. It is a tightly knit Canarian community whose main income is from the sea. The upright young men are tall and proudly good looking, and they work long hard hours. When a boat returns from fishing the whole family and friends rush out to help drag it ashore. Excitedly the children are allowed to look at the catch first. Later they are expected to assist with cleaning out the boat. The fish are put on the beach to be weighed, gutted and sold. Restaurants, hotels, fish-canning factories and family come first, but should there be any left, the tourist may be able to purchase the fish. On occasions the catch is sufficiently large for quantities of fish, usually sardines, to be prepared for drying. It is a laborious task to gut and split open the tiny fish, which are then laid out on wire racks to dry in the sunshine and sprinkled with salt. Later on they are stored in boxes. The Canarians will eat these dried fish raw and consider them a tasty *tappa* (snack).

The fishing village of Las Playitas, a few miles north east of Gran Tarajal. A few apartments are available here.

A small contingent of Scandinavians have bought holiday homes around Las Playitas; they appear to mingle pleasantly with the local community. A bar in the village is very clean and simple meals are available in the restaurant.

The name of **Gran Tarajal** is taken from the tamarisk trees that grow in the area. The town is a busy commercial centre with many shops, supermarkets, garage, cinema, post office and banks. Cafés and bars are found along the seafront, but surprisingly there are no hotels. Its good harbour makes it of great importance to the south of the island; it is second only to Puerto del Rosario for the export of tomatoes, which are grown and packed locally. A large beach has fine blackish sands and a pleasant paved promenade.

Island tour 5

Gran Tarajal — Tarajalejo — Playa de la Pared — Costa Calma — Playa Jandía — Morro Jable — Cofete — Punta de Jandía (about 69 km; ½-day drive)

Two kilometres north of Gran Tarajal a turning left is signposted Tarajalejo and Morro Jable. The road is tarmac but rough in places as it winds its way around Morro Negro and past isolated farmsteads.

On your left you will notice a sign Galerie La Fuentita, the entrance is almost opposite the Bar Rafael. Here in a desert-like setting you find amid palm trees and a windmill a permanent exhibition of original works by the Argentine painter, Alenjandro Andreoni. Working in oil, pastel and water colour his work mostly depicts the local people and landscapes of Fuerteventura. In the same gallery Beatrice Kunz creates wonderful batik and silk work, some in splendid muted tones. The high prices reflect the quality of these talented artists.

Six kilometres from the signpost a turning seawards leads down a *barranco* to the small seafront and quiet beach of **Giniginamar.** A few fishermen's cottages line the shore and ancient *marjoreros* sit in their doorways, while younger members of the family paint their boats and tend the nets. On the side of the hill to the rear of the village a small development of villas and apartments looks very much out of keeping with the quiet scenery. Here, behind a high stone wall, lies what must have been a grand mansion. Its many windows are now shuttered and in a state of disrepair, only a brilliant bougainvillea clinging to the side wall reminds one of past glory.

Back on the main road it is another eight kilometres to Tarajalejo; just before you reach the town you will notice, on the right, El Brasero, which is a ranch-type restaurant. You may enjoy a good meal here, cooked on an open barbecue. While you wait you can have a ride on a horse or camel, which are tethered outside.

The village of **Tarajalejo** is a small Canarian community. A forlorn seafront, from which three or four local fishing boats go out each day, is very neglected. In the village three bars have restaurant space where good fish meals are served. All is simple, with plastic tablecloths, and the atmosphere is mostly Canarian. Price of an average fish dish is 800 pesetas (£4.12). A single supermarket is the only shop in Tarajalejo.

On the edge of the village is the football ground, which is also the venue for Canary wrestling *(lucha Canaria),* which starts at about 1800 hr. A yellow sandy beach lies to the southwest of the village. Behind the seafront is a small tourist development consisting of a hotel and apartments. This isolated and quiet position is favoured mostly by German holidaymakers.

Further on is another new tourist venture, called **Jardmax,** which is a combination of a garden centre, a zoo and a camel park. It is an enterprising set up, very well landscaped and will no doubt be a tourist attraction for children, animal lovers and garden enthusiasts as there are some fascinating cacti. Among the animals are chimpanzees, Shetland ponies, peacocks and a variety of small birds including a cheery parrot who greets you with a Spanish *olá!*

Just before the road reaches the little fishing village of **La Lajita,** there is a splendid panoramic view of the southern part of Fuerteventura. In the distance is the light brown rocky mountain range known as **Las Orejas de Asno** (The Asses' Ears) of which **Pico de Zarza** at 807 m is the highest peak. But it is the vast stretch of sand dunes and golden sandy beaches, with their shallow turquoise waters, which make a lasting impression: a great open space so beautiful and full of peace. At this view point there is a useful restaurant, Cuesta de Pared.

The scenery becomes progressively more desert like as one reaches **Matas Blanca,** nine and a half kilometres south of Tarajalejo. This is the area known as the **Jandía Peninsula.** Many centuries ago a dividing wall marked two separate Guanche kingdoms, Maxorata and Jandía. Today a metal road shows the route across the sand dunes and scrubland, and the glare of the sun on the vast sands reminds us of the closeness of Africa.

A small signpost by the main road marks the road to Playa de la Pared on the west coast; at this point the peninsula is only five kilometres wide.

Across the west coast (windwardside) at **Playa de la Pared** is the Atlantida Club, a small German owned apartment hostel. The Club is in a most isolated position; the coastline is very rocky, and swimming can be dangerous because of strong currents. However good fishing is possible from the rocks, when the sea is not too fierce. Nearby **Playa de Barlovento de Jandía** is without metal roads, except from La Pared. Steep crumbling sandstone cliffs make access to the beaches very difficult. It is advisable to retrace your route to the main road unless you have decided to go by a different route to Pájara. (Once there was only a dusty track, but now it is possible to drive on a new road from La Pared to Pájara, 21 km away. It is a wildly beautiful route through the brown mountains and deep *barrancos,* via Degollada Cha Cabrera, (430m) on a high winding pass, without any sign of habitation, although you may see birds of prey swirling overhead.)

But continuing our tour south we soon reach the **Costa Calma** sign and the beginning of the tourist resorts on the leeward side of the island. Once a remote and sandy desert region, over the past few years this area is quickly turning into a holidaymakers paradise of modern hotels and apartments, for the **Playa de Sotavento de Jandía** has the twenty-two kilometre stretch of unbroken sands for which Fuerteventura is so famed. These vast fine grained sands are mostly deserted except for sea birds that fly over from Africa to feed in the lagoons that are formed at low tide; egrets, sandpipers and curlews can be seen, and in the sand dunes the hoopoe birds make a startling splash of colour.

Only a few yards from the Costa Calma sign, on the land side, is the urbanisation Canada del Rió, where a modern village has been created out of the Sahara-like landscape. Across the road further developments include an enormous new hotel being built for the Iberotel Group, the Playa Fuerteventura. By the Hotel Monica is a water park with two slides, and a snack bar pizzeria, squash and tennis courts. There is a supermarket, too.

At **Playa de la Barca** (79 kilometres from Puerto del Rosario and 15 kilometres south of Gran Tarajal) the three-star hotel Los Gorriones is well signposted and has been built right on the beach, standing out like a white castle. This luxury hotel belongs to the Hotasa group of Spanish hoteliers and is used by package holiday tour operators. It has 326 bedrooms with private bathrooms and balconies (most with sea views), and all the facilities of a modern,

This stunning view is of the wonderful Jandia beach, where miles of isolated soft sands allow you to enjoy nudism.

self-contained hotel, including shops, sports facilities and nightly entertainment. As well as the hotel restaurant there is a separate à la carte restaurant open in the evenings, serving international cuisine.

This is very much a hotel for anyone who requires a quiet and peaceful ambience with comfortable accommodation. The beach is tranquil — ideal for naturist swimming and sunbathing. Below the hotel, on the beach, is a windsurfing school, popular with beginners and enthusiasts.

El Esquinzo, Stella Maris and **Playa Jandía,** further south, all have complexes of apartments and villas, with further developments in various stages of building progress along the coast. Very little traffic makes for pleasant driving, but if it is windy watch out for sand that can obliterate the edges of the road.

At **Playa Jandía** two hotels, the four-star Casa Atlantica and the three-star Robinson Club, are used mainly by German tourists; both are situated close to the beach. A nearby modern shopping complex has a boutique, hairdressing salon, supermarket, souvenir shops and travel agents. Two small bars serve meals: everywhere notices are written in Spanish and German and it is hard to find anyone who will speak English. No cars are allowed to park on the beach or in the sand dunes. A wind surfing school, which operates from the beach at Playa Jandía, is very popular. This part of Fuerteventura has created a real tourist boom, and unfortunately the developers have had little regard for preserving the beautiful coastal scenery. Playa Jandía has become a warren of holiday apartments, bars and restaurants, which are only offset by the marvellous natural sands of the beach.

Three kilometres further along the main road is the fishing village of **Morro Jable,** a larger than average community with improved facilities since the advent of tourists. There is a bank, several large supermarkets, post office, petrol station and garage, so it has much importance. (For similar services it is a 52 kilometre drive to Gran Tarajal.) However there is a need for more parking space, and it may be necessary to leave your transport on the outskirts and walk to the shops and beach.

Morro Jable has a high reputation with tourists for its fish meals. Two cafés have terraces where food may be eaten in the sunshine. A very narrow road leads to the beach, where local fishermen keep their small boats with the nets spread out over the sands. Often the fish are put out to dry, making it a very pictorial scene. The newly built harbour at Morro Jable is designed to become a yacht marina with full facilities. At present it is used by fishing and pleasure craft. It also has a quay for the Trasmediterranea jetfoil that goes daily to Las Palmas in Gran Canaria and Tenerife.

It is possible to walk from Morro Jable to Hotel Los Gorriones, a distance of twenty-one kilometres along the wide sandy beach — a super walk but you will need a rest and a drink afterwards!

Another excursion is to hire a four-wheel drive jeep (not a car) and make the trip from Morro Jable to Playa Cofete across on the Barlovento coast. (It can be walked if you are experienced, as it is about 15 km with a strenuous climb through the Degollada de Cofete pass.) This is a rough bumpy ride through the Barranco Gran Valle, 4.5 km west of Morro Jable. It is along this route that you may see the *euphorbia jandiensis,* which is one of the two endemic and rare plants in Fuerteventura, the other being the cactus *cardoncillo de jandia.*

There is an interesting story about an abandoned house near the hamlet of Cofete. It used to belong to a German who came to the island before the Second World War. He owned all the Jandía peninsula and at one time forbade anyone to live at Cofete, where he built his house. There are mysterious rumours about what happened there.

At Costa Calma in the south of Fuerteventura beach lovers can have an idyllic holiday — except when the wind blows.

You will be pleased to know that near the beach is a small bar restaurant, where you are likely to enjoy a meal of fresh fish. Although Barlovento beach looks inviting for a swim, do be careful as there is a very strong undertow that can be dangerous. Remember, this is the windy side of the island.

At present the tarmac road continues past Morro Jable for just two kilometres along the coast and then a dirt track for 18 kilometres leads to the lighthouse at **Punta de Jandía,** the extreme south west of Fuerteventura; here the cliffs and a rocky beach mark the end of the land.

Finale

Lanzarote and Fuerteventura — here are two islands which are entirely different yet they are less than 20 km apart.

Lanzarote is in many ways an island that evades description. Impressive, widely contrasting, moon-like, sun-drenched — all these phrases are true of its landscape, full of vermilion, ochre, grey, black, blue and gold. It remains a strangely differing sunny island of white sandy beaches and black volcanic lava, with exciting caves and tidy, flat roofed, green and white houses — a wonderful mixture of colourful windsails, games on the beach, walks along steep cliffs and dining in the moonlight. But there is something beyond all this, some extraordinary and mysterious quality that fascinates everyone who comes here and that, after you have left, will make you yearn to return again to the Fire Island of Lanzarote.

Fuerteventura is not a place for those who like bright lights and noisy entertainments on their holiday. There is little to do but swim and sunbathe, unless you are energetic and like to windsurf, fish or enjoy underwater swimming. It is very much a place where one 'gets away from it all', a wonderful land, full of light and mellow colours, of open vistas, where the local people accept the needs of the tourist without resentment, yet continue to retain their own traditions and crafts.

Off the beaten track, Fuerteventura is one of the places where true wilderness remains to be visited by the traveller, an island of solitude.

Spanish/English Vocabulary

Public signs and notices

abierto	open
aseo	toilet
caballeros	gentlemen
cerrado	closed
empuje	push
entrada	entrance
libre	free/vacant
muelle	quay
ocupado	engaged
privado	private
salida	depart/way out
senoras	ladies
se alquilar	to rent
se prohibe	forbidden
servicio	toilet
se vende	for sale
se prohibe estacioner	no parking
se prohibe fumar	no smoking
tire	pull

Drinks

beer	*cerveza*
coffee/black	*café solo*
Coffee/white	*café con leche*
gin	*ginebra*
ice	*hielo*
sherry	*jerez*
squash	*zumo*
tea	*té*
water	*agua*
wine dry	*vino seco*
red	*vino tinto*
sweet	*vino dulce*
white	*vino blanco*

Shops and places

bakery	*panaderia*
butcher's shop	*carnicería*
cake shop	*pastelería*
chemist	*farmacia*
church	*iglesia*
cinema	*cine*
dairy	*lecheria*
fishmonger	*pescadería*
grocer	*alimentacion*
ironmonger	*ferreteria*
library	*biblioteca*
market	*mercado*
post office	*correos*
shoe shop	*zapatería*
stationer	*papeleria*
theatre	*teatro*
town hall	*ayuntamiento*
view point	*mirador*

Restaurant

Bill	*cuenta*
bottle	*botella*
breakfast	*desayuno*
cup	*taza*
dinner	*cena*
drink	*bebida*
fork	*tenedor*
glass	*vaso*
knife	*cuchillo*
lunch	*almuerzo*
plate	*plato*
sandwich	*bocadillo*
spoon	*cuchara*
table	*mesa*
tip	*propina*
waiter	*camarero*

Useful words

all	*todo*
before	*antes*
behind	*detras*
big	*grande*
cold	*frio*
everybody	*todos*
fast	*rapido*
food	*alimento*
good	*bueno*
here	*aqui*
high	*alto*
hot	*caliente*
how many?	*cuantos*
how much?	*cuanto*
left (direction)	*izquierda*
like	*como*
little (quantity)	*poco*
lost	perdido
many	*mas*
near	*cerca*
no	*no*
old	*viejo*
please	*por favor*
right (direction)	*derecha*
slow	*lento*
Soon	*pronto*
thank you	*gracias*
too many	*demasiados*
too much	*demasiado*
under	*debajo*
up	*arriba*
very	*muy*
well	*bien*
when?	*cuando*
why?	*por que*
without	*sin*
with	*con*
yes	*si*

Days of the week

Sunday	*Domingo*
Monday	*Lunes*
Tuesday	*Martes*
Wednesday	*Miercoles*
Thursday	*Jueves*
Friday	*Viernes*
Saturday	*Sabado*

Months

January	*Enero*
February	*Febrero*
March	*Marzo*
April	*Abril*
May	*Mayo*
June	*Junio*
July	*Julio*
August	*Agosto*
September	*Septiembre*
October	*Octubre*
November	*Noviembre*
December	*Diciembre*

Numbers

one	*uno, una*
two	*dos*
three	*tres*
four	*cuatro*
five	*cinco*
six	*seis*
seven	*siete*
eight	*ocho*
nine	*nueve*
ten	*diez*

Food

apple	*manzana*
banana	*platano*
beef	*vaca*
biscuit	*galleta*
bread	*pan*
butter	*mantequilla*
cabbage	*col*
caramel pudding	*flan*
carrots	*zanahorias*
cauliflower	*coliflor*
cheese	*queso*
chicken	*pollo*
chop	*chuleta*
cream	*nata*
cucumber	*pepino*
egg	*huevo*
fish	*pescado*
french beans	*judias verde*
grapes	*uvas*
ham	*jamón*
ice cream	*helados*
lamb	*cordero*
lemon	*limon*
lobster	*langosta*
marmalade	*mermelada*
mushrooms	*setas*
mussels	*mejillónes*
mustard	*mostaza*
oil	*aceite*
olives	*aceitunas*
onions	*cebollas*
orange	*naranja*
peach	melocoton
pear	*pera*
peas	*guisantes*
pepper	*pimienta*
pork	*cerda*
potatoes	*patatas*
rice	*arroz*
salad	*ensalada*
salt	*sal*
sauce	*salsa*
sausages	*chorizo*
shrimps	*gambas*
strawberries	*fresas*
sugar	*azucar*
toast	*tostado*
veal	*ternara*
vegetables	*verduras*
vinegar	*vinagre*

Appendix B
Wind Force: the Beaufort Scale*

B'fort No.	Wind Descrip.	Effect on land	Effect on sea	Wind Speed knots	mph	kph	Wave height (m)†
0	Calm	Smoke rises vertically	Sea like a mirror	less than 1			-
1	Light air	Direction shown by smoke but not by wind vane	Ripples with the appearance of scales; no foam crests	1-3	1-3	1-2	-
2	Light breeze	Wind felt on face; leaves rustle; wind vanes move	Small wavelets; crests do not break	4-6	4-7	6-11	0.15-0.30
3	Gentle breeze	Leaves and twigs in motion wind extends light flag	Large wavelets; crests begin to break; scattered white horses	7-10	8-12	13-19	0.60-1.00
4	Moderate breeze	Small branches move; dust and loose paper raised	Small waves, becoming longer; fairly frequent white horses	11-16	13-18	21-29	1.00-1.50
5	Fresh breeze	Small trees in leaf begin to sway	Moderate waves; many white horses; chance of some spray	17-21	19-24	30-38	1.80-2.50
6	Strong breeze	Large branches in motion; telegraph wires whistle	Large waves begin to form; white crests extensive; some spray	22-27	25-31	40-50	3.00-4.00

7	Near gale	Whole trees in motion; difficult to walk against wind	Sea heaps up; white foam from breaking waves begins to be blown in streaks	28-33	32-38	51-61	4.00-6.00
8	Gale	Twigs break off trees; progress impeded	Moderately high waves; foam blown in well-marked streaks	34-40	39-46	63-74	5.50-7.50
9	Strong gale	Chimney pots and slates blown off	High waves; dense streaks of foam; wave crests begin to roll over; heavy spray	41-47	47-54	75-86	7.00-9.75
10	Storm	Trees uprooted; considerable structural damage	Very high waves, overhanging crests; dense white foam streaks; sea takes on white appearance; visibility affected	48-56	66-63	88-100	9.00-12.50
11	Violent storm	Widespread damage, seldom experienced in England	Exceptionally high waves; dense patches of foam; wave crests blown into froth; visibility affected	57-65	64-75	101-110	11.30-16.00
12	Hurricane	Winds of this force encountered only in Tropics	Air filled with foam & spray; visibility seriously affected	65 +	75 +	120 +	13.70 +

* Introduced in 1805 by Sir Francis Beaufort (1774-1857) hydrographer to the Navy
† First figure indicates average height of waves; second figure indicates maximum height.

APPENDIX C: USEFUL CONVERSION TABLES

Distance/Height

feet	**ft or m**	metres
3.281	1	0.305
6.562	2	0.610
9.843	3	0.914
13.123	4	1.219
16.404	5	1.524
19.685	6	8.829
22.966	7	2.134
26.247	8	2.438
29.528	9	2.743
32.808	10	3.048
65.617	20	8.096
82.081	25	7.620
164.05	50	15.25
328.1	100	30.5
3281.	1000	305.

Weight

pounds	**kg or lb**	kilograms
2.205	1	0.454
4.409	2	0.907
8.819	4	1.814
13.228	6	2.722
17.637	8	3.629
22.046	10	4.536
44.093	20	9.072
55.116	25	11.340
110.231	50	22.680
220.462	100	45.359

Distance

miles	**km or mls**	kilometres
0.621	1	1.609
1.243	2	3.219
1.864	3	4.828
2.486	4	6.437
3.107	5	8.047
3.728	6	9.656
4.350	7	11.265
4.971	8	12.875
5.592	9	14.484
6.214	10	16.093
12.428	20	32.186
15.534	25	40.234
31.069	50	80.467
62.13	100	160.93
621.3	1000	1609.3

Dress sizes

Size	bust/hip inches	bust/hip centimetres
8	30/32	76/81
10	32/34	81/86
12	34/36	86/91
14	36/38	91/97
16	38/40	97/102
18	40/42	102/107
20	42/44	107/112
22	44/46	112/117
24	46/48	117/122

Tyre pressure

lb per sq in	kg per sq cm
14	0.984
16	1.125
18	1.266
20	1.406
22	1.547
24	1.687
26	1.828
28	1.969
30	2.109
40	2.812

Temperature

centigrade	fahrenheit
0	32
5	41
10	50
20	68
30	86
40	104
50	122
60	140
70	158
80	176
90	194
100	212

Oven temperatures

Electric	Gas mark	Centigrade
225	¼	110
250	½	130
275	1	140
300	2	150
325	3	170
350	4	180
375	5	190
400	6	200
425	7	220
450	8	230

Your weight in kilos

stones

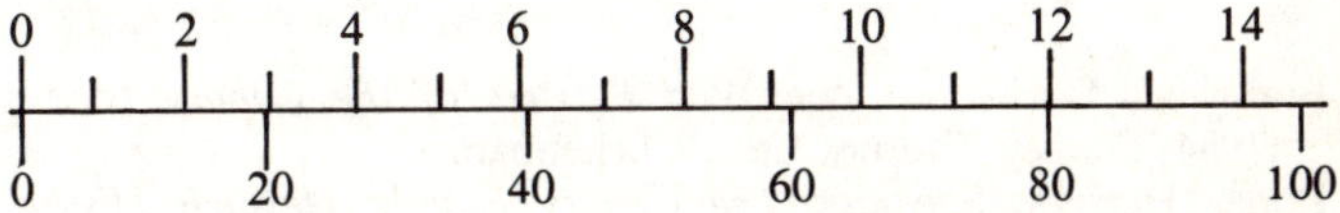

kilograms

Liquids

gallons	**gal or l**	litres
0.220	1	4.546
0.440	2	9.092
0.880	4	18.184
1.320	6	27.276
1.760	8	36.368
2.200	10	45.460
4.400	20	90.919
5.500	25	113.649
10.999	50	227.298
21.998	100	454.596

Some handy equivalents for self caterers

1 oz	25 g	1 fluid ounce	25 ml
4 oz	125 g	¼ pt. (1 gill)	142 ml
8 oz	250 g	½ pt.	284 ml
1 lb	500 g	¾ pt.	426 ml
2.2 lb	1 kilo	1 pt.	568 ml
		1¾ pints	1 litre

Bibliography

Bramwell, David and Zoe *Wild Flowers of the Canary Islands* (1984) Stanley Thornes Ltd., Cheltenham.

Lopez Herrera, Salvador *The Canary Islands Through History* (1978) London.

Myhill, Henry *The Canary Islands* (1968) Faber and Faber, London.

Rochford, Noel *Landscapes of Lanzarote and Fuerteventura* (1989) Sunflower Books, London.

Names of islands abbreviated as follows:
Lanzarote (Lan); Fuerteventura (Fue)

accommodation 23-9
  Fuerteventura 156-8
  Lanzarote 88-90
agriculture 70-1
Agua de Bueyes (Fue) 184
airports and air services
  15-16, 117, 191
Ajuy (Fue) 186
Antigua (Fue) 163
Arrecife capital (Lan) 83, 111-16
  accommodation 88
  nightlife 103
  restaurants 97-9, 114
  tourist office 14
Arrieta (Lan) 146
art galleries *see* museums and
  galleries
Atalaya de Femés (Lan) 126

banks 53-4
bars 43-4
basketwork 77
Betancuria (Fue) 153, 189-90
  restaurants 163
bicycle hire 93
boating 21-2, 107, 168
British Consul 45
budgeting 45
buses 36
  Fuerteventura 159
  Lanzarote 91-2

Cactus Garden (Lan) 147
Caleta de Fuste (Fue) 153, 155, 192
  accommodation 157
  restaurants 163
Caleta del Mojon Blanco (Lan)
  87, 144
Caleta del Sebo (La Graciosa)
  144
Caleta Negra (Fue) 186
Caleton Blanco (Lan) 87, 144
camel rides 130
camping 26-9
Canada del Río (Fue) 197
car hire 35
  Fuerteventura 160-1
  Lanzarote 92-3
car servicing and repairs 35
Casa El Golfo (Lan) 125
Casillas del Angel (Fue) 183
Castillo de las Coloradas (Lan)
  129
Castillo de San Gabriel
  (Arrecife) 112
Castillo de San José
  (Arrecife) 116
Charca de la Lala (Lan) 87, 144
Charcos de San Ginés (Lan) 111
chemists 46
children 55-6
church services 46
climate 11-13
  Fuerteventura 152-3
  Lanzarote 82-3
  wind force chart 206-7
clothes
  to take 46-8, 83, 153
  for purchase 104
complaints 55
concerts 105
conversion tables 208-11
Corralejo (Fue) 153, 177
  accommodation 156
  restaurants 164
Costa Calma (Fue) 197
  accommodation 158
Costa Teguise (Lan) 83, 85, 147
  accommodation 88-9
  nightlife 102
  restaurants 99
Cuevas de los Verdes (Lan) 83,
  144-5
currency 14, 53

dancing, Canarian 74-5
dentists 50
doctors 50, 53
drinks 42-3
driving
  international routes 18
  Spain and islands 33-5

duty free goods 51
El Castillo de Fuste 192
El Cotillo (Fue) 153, 156, 180
  restaurants 164
El Esquinzo (Fue) 198
El Golfo (Lan) 83, 87, 125
El Molino (Fue) 184
El Río (Lan) 143
electricity 51
Embalse de los Molinos (Fue) 191
embroidery 78, 179
Ermita de la Nieves (Lan) 141
estate agents 31
excursions 36-8
  Fuerteventura 161
  Lanzarote 95-6

ferries
  international 16-19
  inter-island 20-1
festivals and fiestas 73-4
Fire Mountain 130-2
fishing 72, 162, 167
flora 66-7
folklore 74
food 39-42

geographical background 10-11
Giniginamar (Fue) 195
golf 107, 147
Gran Tarajal (Fue) 153, 156, 195
Grotto Jameos del Agua (Lan) 84, 145-6
Guanapay, volcano 141
Guatiza (Lan) 147

hairdressers 52
handicrafts 75-8, 114
Haría (Lan) 83, 142
health care 52-3
historical background 59-63
  Fuerteventura 150-2
  Lanzarote 81-2
hospitals 53
hotels *see* accommodation

Isla de Los Lobos 154, 161, 177-9
Islote de Hilario (Lan) 132
Jameos del Agua (Lan) 84, 145-6
Jandia (Fue) 155, 196
Jardmax (Fue) 196
jeep safari 161

La Ampuyenta (Fue) 184
La Antigua (Fue) 184
La Caleta de Famara (Lan) 84, 87, 141
La Geria (Lan) 134
La Graciosa, island 84, 87, 144
La Lajita (Fue) 196
La Oliva (Fue) 154, 180-2
La Santa (Lan) 134
Lajares (Fue) 179
language 65
  vocabulary list 203-5
Las Breñas (Lan) 126
Las Dunas (Fue) 155, 175
Las Nieves (Lan) 141
Las Playitas (Fue) 154, 156, 193
Llano de Zonzamas (Lan) 85, 138
Llanos de la Concepcion (Fue) 191
local dishes 40-2
Los Cocoteros (Lan) 147
Los Hervideros (Lan) 84, 125
Los Limones (Lan) 128
Los Pocillos (Lan) 84
Los Valles (Lan) 141

Mácher (Lan) 120
Mála (Lan) 147
Malpais de la Corona (Lan) 144
Mancha Blanca 134
Manrique, César 15, 78, 80, 105, 114, 116, 130, 136, 138, 143, 147
Matagorda (Lan) 119
Matas Blanca (Fue) 196
medical services 53
Mezquez (Fue) 186
Mirador del Río (Lan) 84, 142
money 53-4
Montaña de Maneje (Lan) 138
Montaña Quemada (Fue) 182
Montaña Tindaya (Lan) 182

Monte Corona (Lan) 142
Monte Mina (Lan) 138
moped hire 93
Morro Jable (Fue) 154, 199
  restaurants 164
Mozaga (Lan) 84, 136
Muñique (Lan) 135
museums and galleries
  Arrecife
    archaeology 105, 112
    art 105, 116
  Betancuria, archaeology 189
  Casa Museo del Campesino 105
  Haria, sacred images 105
  Teguise, art 105
  Yaiza, art 105
music, Canarian 74-5

national holidays 72-3
national parks 67
  see also under name
Nazaret (Lan) 138
needlework 78, 179
newspapers 54
nightlife
  Fuerteventura 164-5
  Lanzarote 101-3
nudist centres 83, 129
Nuestra Senora de los Volcanes (Lan) 134

open threadwork 78
opticians 54
Orzola (Lan) 143

package holidays 30
Pájara (Fue) 154, 185-6
Papagayo (Lan) 84, 128-9
paradors 25-6
Parque Natural de las Dunas de Corralejo (Fue) 67, 154, 175
passports 13
Peña Horadada (Lan) 186
Peñas del Chache (Lan) 79, 141
peridot 125
petrol 34
Pico de la Zarza (Fue) 149
Playa Blanca (Fue) 156
Playa Blanca (Lan) 84, 87, 127
  accommodation 90
  night life 103
  restaurants 100
Playa Cofete (Fue) 199
Playa de Afe (Lan) 129
Playa de Barlovento de Jandia (Fue) 197
Playa de la Arena (Lan) 87
Playa de la Barca (Fue) 197
Playa de la Garita (Lan) 146
Playa de la Pared (Fue) 197
Playa de los Charcos (Lan) 148
Playa de los Pocillos (Lan) 119
Playa de Puerto Muelas (Lan) 129
Playa de Sotavento (Fue) 155
Playa del Cable (Lan) 87
Playa El Motorral (Fue) 192
Playa Famara (Lan) 87, 141
Playa Flamingo (Lan) 87, 128
Playa Garita (Lan) 87
Playa Honda (Lan) 117
Playa Jandía (Fue) 154, 198
Playa Mujeres (Lan) 129
Playa Quemada (Lan) 87, 122
Playa Reducto (Lan) 87, 114
police 54-5
ports 19
post offices 48-9
pottery 77, 136
Pozo Negro (Fue) 156, 193
  restaurants 164
Puertito de los Molinos (Fue) 183
Puerto Calero (Lan) 122
Puerto de la Peña (Fue) 186
Puerto de Naos (Lan) 116
Puerto del Carmen (Lan) 84, 87, 119-20
  accommodation 89-90
  nightlife 101-2
  restaurants 99-100
Puerto del Rosario, capital (Fue) 154, 171-3, 191
  accommodation 157
  restaurants 164
  tourist office 14, 172

Puerto Oliva (Fue) 175
Punta de Jandía (Fue) 201
Punta Mujeres (Lan) 146
Punta Pechiguera (Lan) 128

radio 51
restaurants 43-4
  Fuerteventura 163-4
  Lanzarote 97-101
Riscos de Famara (Lan) 142
roads and road signs 34
  Fuerteventura 158
  Lanzarote 90-1

Salinas de Janubio (Lan) 84, 123
San Bartolomé (Lan) 137-8
Santa Barbara, castle (Lan) 141
Santa Maria de Betancuria (Fue) 153, 189-90
  restaurants 163
scooter hire 93
shopping 103-4, 165
Sóo (Lan) 136
Spanish Consulate (London) 13
Spanish National Tourist Office (London) 13-14
sports 106-10, 167-9
Stella Maris (Fue) 198

Tahice (Lan) 138
Tao (Lan) 136
Tarajalejo (Fue) 197
  accommodation 158
  restaurants 164
taxis 35-6
  Fuerteventura 160
  Lanzarote 92
Tefia (Fue) 183
Teguise (Lan) 84, 138-9
telegraph and telex 50
telephones 49
television 51
Tetir (Fue) 183
Tiagua (Lan) 135
Timanfaya National Park 84, 129-32
time 56
time share 30
Tinajo (Lan) 134
Tindaya (Fue) 182
tipping 56
Toto (Fue) 185
tourist information offices 13-14
tourist season 13
travel agents 29
Tuinje (Fue) 185

Uga (Lan) 122

Vega de Río de Palma (Fue) 189
visas 13

walking 109, 168
water 57
water sports 109-10, 168-9
weaving 78
wildlife 68
wines 42
wrestling, Canary 94

yachting 21-2, 107, 168
Yaiza (Lan) 85, 122-3
Ye (Lan) 143

Zonazamas Ruins (Lan) 85, 138